Game Fishing:
Methods and Memories

Game Fishing: Methods and Memories

C. W. K Mundle

BARRIE & JENKINS
COMMUNICA - EUROPA

First published in 1978 by
Barrie and Jenkins Ltd
24 Highbury Crescent, London N5 1RX

ISBN 0 214 20560 6

Photoset, printed and bound
in Great Britain by
REDWOOD BURN LIMITED
Trowbridge & Esher

For Jim

and our many benefactors

'Fishing is unquestionably a form of madness, but, happily, for the once-bitten there is no cure.' (Lord Home).

'No-one can look back over days of recreation with more certain gratitude than he who has had the opportunity of fly fishing, and has been born with the gift of enjoying angling.' (Viscount Grey).

'A day spent fishing is not deducted from the span of your life.' (Attributed to Confucius).

Acknowledgements

I thank the editors of *Trout and Salmon, The Field, Rod and Line* and *The Scotsman* for permission to use material previously published in their journals. I am indebted to Mr. T. V. Winsor's skill as a physiotherapist which made it physically possible for me to write this book. Mrs. Kitty Stevens has helped me by typing and sometimes criticising what I had written, deciphering which was, however, her greatest achievement. Being unable to re-visit with my camera many of the waters of which I write, I have sought and received generous help from several expert photographers, notably Arthur Oglesby, Steve Wallace and Cowper of Perth. My greatest debt, however, is to owners of fishing rights who have kindly permitted me to share their privilege. I am grateful to my friend John Pollard for his help in checking the proofs.

The drawings are by Colin Gibson, except for that on page 77 by Norman Thelwell reproduced from *The Compleat Tangler* (Methuen & Co. Ltd).

C.W.K.
Ashcliffe
Dunning
Perthshire

Contents

List of Half-tone Illustrations

Introduction

Having derived so much pleasure and profit from books about game fishing, I have long hoped to add one to this large pool. Given the opportunity, this book drafted itself with surprising speed. It is not, however, the book that I had envisaged – wistful nostalgic memories plus solemn debates about tackle and technique. Only Part One had been drafted when someone lent me Norman Thelwell's *Compleat Tangler*. This led me to recognise situational humour in some of the experiences due to be described. At the time of those events I had been much too busy fishing to *laugh* about fishing. But now I cannot promise, as William Stewart did at the start of his fishing book, that a reader 'will certainly find nothing amusing.' If other dedicated anglers feel that my book is too light-hearted, Thelwell is indirectly responsible; but I, for one, am grateful for his gift of provoking laughter.

After this book had been drafted, an article about angling literature appeared in *Trout and Salmon* (December, 1976). Mr. H. F. Wallis expressed therein distaste for instruction presented in textbook style, adding: 'I like my education to be improved in more subtle and enjoyable ways . . . The author who manages to inform me about tackle and techniques in the course of an enthralling if quite imaginary account of a fishing expedition . . . will win my devotion.' I share his taste, and hope that this book would meet with his approval, despite the fact that in my fishing stories I have not had to draw on my imagination, only on memory. As a consumer of fishing books I am however omnivorous.

I share Patrick Chalmers' view that, though some are better than others, 'all fishing books are naturally good.' I rush through how-to-catch-them books in search of wrinkles which may make me less incompetent. For example, Hugh Falkus's excellent manual *Sea-trout Fishing*, so well adapted to increase one's productivity.

Especially when I am not able to wield a rod, I browse again in books like those by Chalmers and Harry Plunket Greene – both for their lyricism and humour, and for enabling me to imagine fishing waters which I have not fished in reality. I find even more appetising books which combine new ideas about technique and vivid descriptions of days by, on, or in the water, like those of G. P. R. Balfour-Kinnear.

I have never required humour, but I value it as a bonus. Fishing books might be classified according to whether they make you laugh (A) with the author, (B) at the author, or (C) not at all. I shall not mind if this book provokes a bit of (B), if it achieves a little of (A). I am not, of course, criticising what I label class (C) works. There is an important place for texts, which, in a sober and systematic manner, provide instruction about rods and flies and how to use them; and also for less didactic books which discuss problems of fishy psychology. For example, from what motive(s) do salmon take our lures? I shall not discuss this question since it seems impossible to verify any answer. Nor shall I debate another well-worn question: whether the salmonidae have colour vision, since it has been verified by scientists that they do.

I do not, of course, require that a fishing book should tell us directly about the man behind the rod; but some of my favourites do disclose some of their authors' other interests and activities. I have usually found this a bonus. Not always – for example in some Victorian books whose authors competed to produce the longest subtitle. Still, Gavin Maxwell's books would be impoverished if he had told us only about the otters and other wild creatures which he tamed, and how. Similarly, I think, fishing books like those of Greene, Sir Robert Bruce Lockhart, A. R. B. Haldane and Negley Farson would be impoverished had they written only about the fish they caught, and how. I offer this as an excuse for a few short digressions from the activity of angling, including even a little philosophising.

For me the spice of fishing, like that of living, is variety. Hoping to illustrate the pleasures to be derived from variety in angling, I shall start, egotistically, by indicating the range of my fishing experience – negligible compared with that of some like Augustus Grimble, but apparently wider than that of the authors of some very good books.

1
Down Memory Lane

Beginnings

Some people fish because it is a traditional part of their way of life. My innate impulse must have been a throwback as none of my known ancestors had any interest in (unless disapproval of) blood-sports. My mother said that she found me, when aged three, dangling a piece of string on a cane over the banisters, 'fishing'. Did I get the idea from some bedtime story? A few years later, my first fishing adventure took place on the pier at Broughty Ferry when using a hand-line baited with a mussel to catch 'podles' as we called them. I fell in, could not swim, and the tide was drawing me away from the pier, though I clutched a fishing line thrown by a fellow angler. Fortunately a larger boy did some life-saving. I have a vivid memory of pushing a dripping zigzag course back up the pier, unnoticed by the host of fisher-folk rushing in the opposite direction with shouts of 'Drowning boy', 'He's sunk three times', etc.

My first taste of trout fishing was magic. My parents were persuaded to let their ten-year-old stay up late and hold a fly rod in the stern of the boat while others did some serious fly fishing at dusk on Loch Ericht. There were flies on my rod too, and the breeze made casting unnecessary. I was absorbed by the moon rising over the mountains when the miracle happened: a trout attached itself firmly to one of my flies. From then on, I was hooked. My father bought me, for £1, a greenheart fly rod from Hardy's. A good rod, and it still is, though one of the top pieces became shortened by a pike. It served as my only rod for twenty years.

I have had the luck to enjoy for half a century an era of freedom for Scottish anglers. Soon after catching that first trout I was solemnly informed by a Minister of the Kirk that in Scotland trout fishing is free fishing; and in this respect at least he practised what he preached. I believed him implicitly, having been brought up to revere Churchmen. I felt that I had divine authority when helping myself to Highland trout for many ensuing years. It was over twenty years later before I learnt that according to the Law, that Minister, though correct about practice, was not quite correct about legal theory. Though I doubt whether it has actually happened, an owner could prosecute a boy for using a trout rod – though only after going through cumbersome legalities – taking out an 'interdict' forbidding him to fish that particular water again. But now we have the Freshwater and Salmon Fisheries Act (Scotland), 1976, which will make it possible in future for an unauthorised trout fisher to be prosecuted.

During my later schooldays, when condemned to live in that fog-bound city, I often day-dreamed about trout at Glasgow Academy, especially during Latin lessons. My Latin master forgave me. He organised the school's angling outing to Loch Ard, and twice rowed a boat for me! There, at least, I did not let him down: one year I won the prize – with the only trout caught. Summer holidays, often in Blair Atholl, were what I then lived for. As an angler I was self-taught, at least, if you do not count the valuable teaching conveyed in books; for I read everything I could find on the subject in public libraries.

In those happy days before the Hydro-Electric Board killed the Garry, before Wanless's harmful work in publicising spinning for trout, it was a splendid trout stream. The mile or two below the village comprised not salmon pools but rippling shallows, shaded with greenery. Despite my crude technique – wading bare-legged and casting down and across, I caught good trout on little spiders, including one of 1½ lb taken in blazing sunshine. And there were in the Garry a lot of big cannibal trout, liable to grab a small fish when one was winding it in. Sometimes they would hang on to their prey until almost (but never quite) in reach of the landing net.

I discovered the moorland reaches of the River Bruar up above the Falls, where I was disturbed only by capercaillies clattering out of the firs on the far bank. In those days it was full of innocent trout of up to ¾ lb, glad to grab an up-stream wet fly. Only once did I meet another angler there. He had fished the Bruar for fifty years, but his creel was not very much fuller than mine. I had better warn you that the Hydro-Electric Board has destroyed this river too. On one occasion, my worried father met me near the Falls at dusk. I had been fishing since breakfast on an empty stomach. He carried my load of trout back to the car in silence. I think it was a case of relief suppressing indignation.

Another vivid memory. I had fished up the Girnaig burn to the base of Beinn a'Ghlo and filled my creel. When walking down the winding burn, a huge bird soared from behind a nearby knoll with a smaller bird in its talons. On seeing me it dropped its prey and sailed away. Lying dead on the heather was a large hawk – for then, to me, a hawk was just a hawk. As I later learned from bird books, it was a peregrine falcon. Then I knew that I had seen an eagle. Is it not rare for raptors to prey upon raptors? I have not since read or heard of an eagle killing a peregrine, but it seems rather late for a letter to *The Field*.

In my last school holiday, I had conveyed the bug to my twelve-year-old brother Jim, who could now cast a fly as well as I did. Our expeditions ranged wider. In one energetic day we cycled to and from Dalwhinnie (about fifty far from flat miles), returning at midnight with trout from Loch Ericht *and* Loch Garry, where we had arrived for the 'evening rise'. But our favourite loch, still my dream loch, was more accessible. It nestles in the heather near the base of a massive mountain. Half-way along the west shore there is a wooded promontory around which the best trout lay. We fished it profitably half a dozen times without meeting a soul. On the last afternoon of the holiday, we were surprised as we fished to see a procession of people and pony-traps wending down the track from the mountain towards Blair Atholl. (It was the shooting party returning from the higher moors.) After another ten minutes of carefree fishing I was startled to find that silently there had materialised behind me an enormous red-bearded man of terrifying aspect. At first he seemed too apoplectic to find any words. I think the first were 'Empty that creel'. His eyes goggled when he saw the contents; more so when he found that Jim, in his short trousers, had as many trout as I did. He thawed sufficiently to inspect our casts and ask what flies we had been catching most of them on. Then, remembering his role, off he marched with our re-filled creels and orders to report to him at the mansion. On re-meeting him, his eyes twinkled a bit. He tried to look fierce when he admonished us, but he let us keep half the trout. This was generous. We had embarrassed a head keeper by fishing the tenants' water under their noses.

During my student days at St. Andrews, fishing took a back seat, due to other preoccupations, emotional distractions and the need to earn during vacations because of my father's death. Then came the war. Six years in the RAF provided a mixture of excitement, boredom and intellectual starvation. Still, it was in an Officers' Mess that I found a fellow Scot, Sheila, who hooked me that first evening with accounts of her explorations of the darkest Highlands. (The story which I remember concerned her shock and the eeriness of being aroused from sleep by a stag which gave its rutting roar just outside her tent in a remote and deserted glen.) During these years I suffered increasingly from withdrawal symptoms due to deprivation of fishing. I thrice sought relief, abortively if you judge by Falkus's view that all that matters to an angler is his catch.

Firstly, while in Ulster I got permission to have an evening on a private lough of high repute. I used some of the country's precious petrol to get myself there, beheld it dimpled with rising fish – then found that I had forgotten my reel! (More recently I arrived for a week's fishing on the Dee and found that my suitcase had been left in Edinburgh. Being an absent-minded philosopher can be inconvenient.)

The second time was during the last two years of the war. I was stuck with a staff job at Whitehall where everyone worked at snail's pace, exhausted by the excessive hours throughout which Churchill required us to be on call. Each June I told my Wing-Commander that I *must* have a cast or bust, and he, kind man, arranged for me to make an unnecessary visit of inspection to a Scottish radar station. The first time I headed for a hotel in Blair Atholl. I had just 'phoned the laird, who had said that I was welcome to spend the morrow on that dream loch. I entered the bar for a celebratory drink. Whom should I bump into but my Group Captain from the Air Ministry, a man noted for his hot temper! 'What the hell are you doing here?' is what I expected. Fortunately he was in a mellow mood, celebrating the capture of some Garry salmon. Both in mufti, we happily talked fishing. No questions were asked. I wondered later if he too was officially elsewhere.

Next morning a surprise – the red-bearded giant awaited me at the boathouse. He did not remember me and I thought that it would be tactless to remind him of our earlier meeting. I was treated as an honoured guest. He worked the boat diligently all day. I never had a rise, but his courtesy and company made that tolerable. As we parted, he said that I was welcome to return after dinner in case there was an evening rise. There wasn't, but something more surprising. I was lying on the bank in the twilight awaiting the rise, miles from human beings as I thought. Who should appear but a dear friend from St. Andrews days. He was now a chaplain to the Canadian Forestry Corps, who were then felling our woods and bombing our rivers (and also perhaps Loch Moraig?) He had chanced to see my name in the hotel register and set out to find me. We talked until the sky had started to get lighter. He then left, but I still could not tear myself away. The air was warm and there *might* be an early morning rise. There wasn't. But the dawn chorus from the curlews made up for that. I felt whole again as I walked the few miles to my bed, among mountains lit by early sunshine.

My third abortive fishing expedition occurred next June. My visit of inspection left barely time for a day's fishing but I had decided to fulfil a boyhood dream. Alec Maclennan, who first took me out on Loch Ericht, had often told me that in his youth he used to visit a fabulous lochan about 3,000 feet up, under the summit of Ben Alder. He had done this by using an out-board motor to reach the south end of twenty-mile Loch Ericht, then climbed the shoulder of the Ben, and returned invariably with a *sackful* of trout. 'Herring-sized,' he always said, when I asked him how big they were. I believed him implicitly, if only because, having blown off his left hand when an ancient gun blew up, he could simultaneously manage a boat *and* fly fish efficiently. The name of this remote loch had acquired a mystique for me. 'Loch na Pyulach Pay' he pronounced it. (Loch a Bhealaich Bheithe is the spelling on Ordnance maps.) Arriving late at Dalwhinnie, the hotel promised me an early breakfast and the loan of a bicycle. At 7 a.m. I was off on the track to Ben Alder Lodge. I had to leave the cycle in the heather near Loch Pattack (where, as I knew, it was too easy to catch trout of three or four to the pound).

It was a hot day and during the long climb, I found how much out of training I was. I still had the energy to run the last few hundred yards when the lochan came into view – an azure gem below the rugged cliffs which gird the summit. Conditions were perfect: a south-west zephyr and trout visibly feeding. With trembling hands I mounted my tackle. I had not long to wait before I caught the first, a silvery dace-like trout of about seven inches – duly returned. A few minutes later, another exactly like it. It gradually dawned on me that perhaps the loch was full of these, and held nothing else. This suspicion had become a conviction about three hours and fifty fish later. I kept the best five, totalling about one pound. Late that evening, having missed the hotel dinner, I presented my catch to Alec with the mildly reproachful comment that I preferred my herring a bit bigger. He consoled me with food and drink.

From trout to salmon

The RAF gave me an early release to take up my scholarship to Oxford – on the day before term started. Oxford was not ready for us veteran students, as many dons were not back from their battlefields or desks. There were no introductory courses. It was in at the deep end for those starting on new subjects – Economics in my case. My temporary Economics tutor who was blind did not realise that there was a limit to the number of tomes that a beginner with sight could, in half a week, digest and evaluate in a ten-minutes-to-read essay. The other half weeks were easier – essays in Philosophy in which I was not a beginner. But the latter normally went unheard and unread. When my temporary tutor remembered to turn up, usually he had time only to plead some more pressing engagement, and set another essay. It was a strain. I had to get a First. The dreaming spires left me cold. I was recurrently afflicted with an unidentified bug which left me limp. A long summer rest was what I needed.

Some rest! Brother Jim was released by the RAF in May of 1946, and we planned a fishing bonanza to make up for over six years of frustration. It was a blazing June so we usually fished while others slept. Starting at Loch Leven we worked our way north, fishing all of our favourite lochs in Perthshire; and then further north, adding more to our repertoire, with a bias for those most remote. I was irrationally attracted by lochs in proportion to the square of their inaccessibility. Sometimes it has paid off. There is a remote loch in Assynt where the fat trout are apple-green with vivid red spots; and a little lochan in the Grampians with an enormous nesting site of black-cap gulls, nearly 2,000 feet above sea level. They squawk around you all day. I suppose it is the lime from their droppings which results in the Loch Leven sized trout. Find these lochs if you can. I do not intend to make them tourist centres. For most of June we slept in the heat of the afternoon, fished from sundown until midnight or later, lay on the heather and drowsed, and fished the hour before dawn (though the early 'morning rise' was not as rewarding as it is cracked up to be). We gave away trout by the bucketful, sometimes in exchange for a night in a real bed.

When we arrived at the house in Grantown on Spey which our mother had rented for July, my plan was to relax and read. We were very brown, but very thin. We had been 'making a toil o' a pleesure', a local matron said. I had not allowed for the lure of the Spey, the first big river which I was to fish. There was a splendid run of seatrout that summer, averaging well over two pounds. My first encounter was a complete surprise. I was casually throwing a team of loch flies across a shallow run above the old bridge. I nearly fell into the river when the reel screamed and went on screaming until my backing was nearly exhausted and the silver fish started its aerial acrobatics in mid-stream. I expected the light trout cast to break at each of the fish's leaps; but despite its obstinacy in the fast water, gentleness was rewarded and a fresh-run fish of 2½ lb finally slid into the net.

Then for the next three weeks we were at it again, fishing by day when we got the shrunken river to ourselves. We each averaged a sea-trout a day, and were well pleased. Rather small trout flies and 5-lb nylon succeeded even in bright sunshine. Jim, the businessman of the family, traded most of them for prime steak, until I reached the point when I could scarcely look a steak in the face. One had to join a queue when the locals turned out in the evening. We learned why just before the floods of the last week. Jim had invested in a pair of breast waders and he demonstrated their value. We went to the left bank of the Slates Pool, then the bottom pool on the Association water. We were delighted to find all of our many rivals on the other bank. Jim, covering mid-stream, got six, ending with a six pounder. I, from the bank, reaching the water down which he kept wading, naturally got none.

The last week was spoilt by big floods – spoilt for us, that is, not for the locals. Everyone, it seemed, had downed tools and was worming: a method which I thought any fool could practise successfully. More fool me. For the first few days we joined various processions of men and boys walking worms down the edge of the brown water, a few yards apart. They hauled in their fish without ceremony. We watched the piles of seatrout beside their creels growing. I did not get even a nibble. Jim caught one. We gave up in disgust, and when the floods subsided, the seatrout had all run through. Since then I have been a seatrout addict and have plied the art on scores of rivers and lochs. I later learnt to catch them even on worm – though less for pleasure than to satisfy myself that I, too, could do it. Inevitably my thoughts turned towards salmon, but that aspiration took time to fulfil.

Next summer, when the Oxford examination results were announced, I was offered a Professorship in Economics somewhere abroad, but I did not pause to ask in which university, or country, for I had just been offered a lectureship in Philosophy in Dundee. (It was the subject and place, as well as the angling opportunities, which determined my choice.) For the next eight years I had the good fortune to live within range of an abundance of first class fishing. After a prolonged visit to British Columbia, Jim settled in Dundee, and we fished together again. For trout one was spoilt for choice – Loch Leven, Lintrathen or Crombie Reservoir, each much less than an hour's drive away, and lots of lovely hill-lochs for the more energetic days. In one dawn-to-midnight foray we 'did' Loch Tilt, though only two hours of fishing time could be squeezed in. If you look at the map of Scotland *and* the right one-inch maps, you will see why. Jim was a bit cross. I enjoy hill-walking. For him, it was endured as a means to an end – in this case the end was the 3-lb trout that I had promised him. The two dozen which we caught ran three *to the* pound. It later dawned on me that I must have misheard the chattersome old angler who recommended the expedition. He was resting on the bank of the Tay while I was wading in chattering water, concentrating mainly on rising trout.

After the first happy July at Grantown, I devoted the next two Easter holidays to the catching of my first salmon. We stayed with Sheila's Aunt Bessie at Carrbridge, and she, knowing my goal, presented me with a Grantown salmon fishing permit. This obliged me to persevere. I did, but each holiday was a course in aversion therapy (like getting an electric shock whenever you light another cigarette). Day after day I suffered the monotony of hurling ironmongery into the Spey, no doubt in the wrong places, sorting out over-runs in my inefficient revolving drum reel, catching naught but a foolish finnock or two. I never saw a salmon. At the end of each week I escaped from this drudgery by visiting some loch where one could be sure of some flurries of excitement. I felt quite cured of the urge to catch salmon. Before next Easter I told Aunt B that I would not be wanting a salmon permit. Ironically, I caught five salmon that year, all by accident.

In late March, it was still winter on Speyside – the lochs were frozen and the Spey full of snow-water. At a loose end, I accepted a farmer's invitation to try for the big cannibal trout in the deep slow pool by his home. No-one could have known from looking at it that it was a holding pool for salmon. I now used a fixed spool spinning reel, with 5-lb nylon, and the smallest of natural minnows on mounts with tiny hooks. The farmer was right – I soon had three large trout. Then a salmon! But alas, it proved to be a kelt, duly returned. Then another which was as sluggish to play as the kelt, though more obstinate. To my delight, when it came ashore, it was a beautiful blue-backed 8-lb salmon, not long out of the sea. And a few casts later I hooked, and played with much more care, its twin. There were no repeat performances on subsequent visits. Fresh fish in March above Carrbridge were rare events indeed.

The next two accidents happened on the Tay while fishing for sea-trout with university friends who had an open invitation. In June, in thin water, I hooked on a Butcher what seemed to be a strong sea-trout, but turned out to be a little grilse. In August, on my birthday, I stuck to the fly rod, though the flood made it spinning water. Two heavy pulls had felt suspiciously like salmon. I was about to give up when the third pull came, and the Peter Ross stayed put. It was an exciting fight, a big grilse in very strong water, on my ten-foot rod, and nowhere to beach it. The front edge of my landing net met its centre of gravity, and it was touch and go which way it would slide, but the Lord gave me a birthday present. Driving home I was so euphoric that I drove obliviously through red traffic lights – and got fined.

I shall describe the fifth accident in 1949, much as I recorded it, in *Trout and Salmon*, August 1957:

It happened at Lochinver where I was spending a week, late in September, fishing for trout in the hill lochs. The weather was cold and wet and the trout were proving dour, so I was delighted when another resident in the hotel took pity on me and asked me to spend an afternoon with him catching a few salmon in the River Kirkaig. That turbulent stream was running at a good height and we set out full of confidence. I soon got used to the feel of the twelve-foot Grant rod which my benefactor had lent me. As we fished down the lower beat, taking alternative pools, my new friend gave me much useful advice on the salmon lies and how best to work the one and a half inch fly across them. It seemed impossible that all these attractive pools should yield no sport, but our efforts went unrewarded. I had been reading about A. H. E. Wood's techniques in Jock Scott's book, and as we neared the end of the beat I suggested trying a smaller fly. My friend assured me that Wood's methods had been tried and found useless on both the Kirkaig and the Inver rivers.

It was nearly seven o'clock when we got back to the hotel, rather disconsolate. Only then did I remember that two hotel residents from Glasgow had invited me to meet them that evening at the New Pool on the Inver to try to catch a seatrout. They had rented the salmon fishing on the Inver that day. (Normally it was not let by the day, but for some reason, the tenant had left early.) I decided that there was still time to try for a seatrout, so, despite the warnings of my companion of the afternoon that I was wasting my time, I dispensed with food and dashed off with my trout rod. I took it for granted that the others would be fishing the *north* side of New Pool. This is the obvious side for seatrout, since there one casts across shallower and quieter water to the main current which runs close to the south bank.

I found them fishing off the croys on the south side, and it then seemed too late for them to walk round by the bridge. As I put up my rod, we shouted to each other across the river and they told me their tale of woe – several fish (I think it was three) had broken their casts that day, and they were still 'clean'. I mounted a team of flies which had already accounted for many seatrout, with a No. 6 Butcher on the tail, a No. 8 Peter Ross in the middle, and a No. 10 Zulu on the bob. It was still too light, I decided, to fish the lower half of the pool where the bulk of the seatrout would be lying, so I started at the neck of the run. I had not yet got a full line out when it happened. The back of a salmon (it looked as big as a porpoise) broke the surface on the inside edge of the rough water and a dead weight like a log pulled my rod down.

This was it, the long anticipated moment. At last I had hooked a real salmon on fly – and I could not have been less prepared for it. My cast was of 6-lb nylon, I had no gaff and no-one to help me, and at this height of water there appeared to be nowhere that a salmon could possibly be beached. I was not given much time to contemplate my predicament, for the fish woke up and tore off down the pool. Stumbling along the heathery bank I followed as best I could. I have never been less in control of a fish than I was for the next twenty minutes. Fortunately, it chose to conduct a dignified campaign in the middle reaches of the pool, so I was able to maintain a steady, if modest, side-strain on it, sufficient to provoke it into making many short runs. Unfortunately for my friends, it kept moving up and down the water just below the croys from which they were trying to fish. When at last the fish abandoned the support of the main current and started circling more closely to me, an unexpected diversion was caused by a seatrout of about a pound which took my middle fly and started to splash on the surface.

When this fish was beginning to calm down – believe it or not but I had witnesses! – the line started twitching again. A trout of 6 or 8 oz. had affixed itself to my bob fly. For the next few minutes I was in the remarkable position of simultaneously playing a trout and a seatrout as well as a salmon. Not that I was much interested in the former two, which hung in the air or flapped on the surface as the salmon cruised around close to the bank. I had no regrets when the smaller ones were shaken off.

By now the salmon was almost exhausted, and many times it came within gaffing distance. For about fifteen minutes (they seemed endless) I tried to manoeuvre the obstinate beast into a tiny bay where a foot of gravel shelved down, the only place where it might have been persuaded to lie on its side. The snag was a high fence a couple of feet from the water. When I lifted my rod high enough to clear it, the pull on the fish was from too high an angle to force it in. At last I decided that there was nothing for it but to step into two feet of water and try to lift the fish out.

I had read that a handkerchief round one's hand is necessary to get a good grip of a salmon's tail. (This is an old wives' tale.) I wrapped my hanky round my left hand and stepped into the river. The salmon, alarmed, ran off up-stream – straight into the middle of a tangle of weeds! It came to a halt in the middle of it and rolled over onto its side. With desperate haste I slithered up the bed of the river. The droppers must have got caught up. One more flick of its tail and that fish had won its freedom. Would it wait? It did – a bar of silver in the dark water. I carried it far up the bank before laying it down in the bog myrtle – a thick-set, 16-lb cock fish; pretty red I must admit, but, to my eyes, as handsome a fish as I had ever gazed at, not that I could see it very clearly then, for it was almost dark. The hook, I found, had already dropped out of its mouth. It was my lucky day, and just to prove it, I went back for a final cast and within a minute was playing a lively 2½ lb seatrout, which duly came to the net.

My luck must have made it harder for my friends to bear theirs. They did not have an offer all evening. If they felt any envy they did not show it. Still, if they did not have the excitement of catching it, they did at least get the salmon to take back to Glasgow next day. And if their wives were not informed of the precise details of its capture, I should not blame them. That episode taught me an important lesson – take it with a grain of salt when you are told 'the salmon in *this* river will not take small flies.' I have since [i.e. in 1957] confirmed the efficacy of the greased line technique in several rivers in the North-West Highlands, and indeed have yet to find a river where it will not catch salmon.

This section would be incomplete without describing my first salmon caught on fly by design, not accident. Taking Wood of Cairnton as my authority, I acquired my first twelve-foot Grant Vibration rod, a No. 4 Kingfisher line with Mucilin to make it float, and a range of Low Water flies in three of Wood's favourite patterns – Blue Charm, Logie and Blue and Silver. Then I waited impatiently for the chance to apply his technique. It came during 'swot week' – the gap between teaching and examining at the end of May. The first night at Carrbridge I set the alarm at a very early hour, and waited for ages (it seemed) for the kettle to boil before remembering that Aunt B always switched the cooker off at the mains. My impatience was unnecessary. When I got to the pool where I had caught my accidental brace of springers, there was still mist on the water. (Incidentally I now had permission from the rightful owner and not just the *laissez-faire* farmer.)

It was still quite dark when the mist cleared and I started wading inch by inch to avoid rippling the smooth water. When I had a full line out I could see only the nearer half of it. I had almost reached the limit of the wadeable water when the visible part of my line stopped moving, *slowly* straightened, and then the rod bent. It happened so slowly that I remembered to curb my impulse to strike. The fight was on and my heart remained in my mouth for a long time. I must have taken several minutes to the pound. Nearly all of my line was in the river at one stage when the fish was down near the streamy tail, and for the first time I felt that alarming vibration when a fat fly line oscillates in the current. This was a fish I could not bear to lose; and I didn't. When it lay on the bank, the sun had just appeared above the Cromdale hills. I lay back and rejoiced with the darling buds of May. Colours are so intense to dark-adapted retinas. Uncharacteristically, I did not have another cast. I didn't need another fish. I did need a second breakfast. Oddly enough I have never since caught a salmon shortly before dawn, though I have tried not a few times.

The silvery Tay

As a salmon river the Tay deserves all the superlatives, and it holds besides lots of fat trout and some large grayling. Seatrout too, of course, though I have found them rather elusive when they were my quarry. It was pursuit of them, however, which led me to meet and chat with other summer anglers, many of whom, to my surprise, were throwing a big fly thirty or forty yards across the river with the help of their grandfathers' salmon rods. In those days, according to W. J. M. Menzies, an eighteen-foot rod was fit only for 'a comparatively puny man'. From them I learnt that on many lower beats salmon fishing was a traditional privilege of the local, and some not so local, anglers – from the end of the spring fishing (about mid-May) until the end of the estuary netting (on 20 August); provided that one avoided the sin of fishing water soon to be fished by 'the boat', if an occasional owner or guest turned out for a try.

This fact I later confirmed with the head water bailiff, Mr. MacRae, an amiable man who appeared very rarely and only to say 'No spinning', and, if he liked you, to offer advice about flies and lies. He held that fly fishers could do his work on the Tay, leaving his staff free to pursue the poachers who used no rods on tributaries like the Isla and Ericht.

During the earlier part of the twentieth century the Tay was preeminently a spring river, and presumably summer fishing was unprofitable. But already in 1949 the pattern was changing – a decline in the spring runs and an increase in the summer fish – big fish as well as grilse. It astonished me that many lower beats were not let until the nets came off. On my evidence things had changed since Grimble wrote, in 1899: 'what is practically the last heavy run of fish takes place with the Lammas floods, which generally come some time in the first half of August.' But the change was that they continued to run until the season ended; heavy runs still occurred with the first floods of August, and with the help of floods or freshets they started earlier.

Jim and I gladly accepted this gift from the gods. We explored other beats, but we came more and more to concentrate on Cargill/Ballathie and Stobhall/Taymount. (These, with Islamouth, were rightly described by Grimble as 'the cream of the Tay'.) The double-barrelled title, in each case, refers to estates on opposite banks. An owner divides his fishery into an upper and a lower beat, and a fishing party has both banks of a beat, taking upper and lower on alternate days. Nowhere else could one find such a generous day's ration – a mile or so, sometimes more, of a river over 100 yards wide. This lavish system originated from the traditional method of 'harling'. You need a lot of river to spend a day in a boat trolling back and forth across the main stream, covering the main lies only once, or, at most, twice.

So far as I know, I was the first of the summer free fishers to apply Wood's greased line tactics on the Tay. But not before I had tested the then accepted method, which was to use a fly sized 1 to 2/0, almost always a Wilkinson on a single iron. And, of course, the local anglers were right. This was productive, especially in strong streams and in the evening. But I also used a small dropper, persuaded by Anthony Crossley's argument that it helps one to find the preferred size of fly. I expected the dropper to catch only the odd grilse. To my surprise, it caught its share of big fish. This led me to go the whole hog and use Wood's Low Water single irons in the tail position.

The Tay salmon behaved for me as the Dee fish had for Wood. With one's flies just below the surface, fish often swirled up for close inspection without touching, and sometimes at least proved themselves fastidious about the precise size of the fly, by taking the same pattern one size smaller. For me, this is the most exciting moment which salmon fishing can provide – that elongated fraction of a second between seeing the swirl and seeing whether or not the line straightens and a pull follows. (Why do makers of plastic floating lines deprive anglers of this thrill by designing them so that the last few feet *sink*?)

A very good fly fisher, who has fished the Tay for as long as I have, believes that the fish which you catch on little flies are the settled fish, and that those which take fairly big flies are those which pause while running, or the newly arrived. Though cautious of generalising, I think that there is some truth in this. The foot of the Aldern* Stream, on Upper Stobhall, is a place where new arrivals regularly show themselves. The top stretch of the same stream is a place where fish creep up and show inside the edge of the current, when, at dusk, they are preparing to run. I have often taken fresh-run fish ('tide-ies') in both places by changing to a big (No. 1) fly, when small flies (and others' ironmongery) have been used to no avail. I then hedge my bets, however, by retaining the little dropper. And sometimes a big fish takes it, after rejecting the tail fly, when you would think it too dark for anything but a seatrout.

One of the charms, I found, in using little Low Water flies was that, wind permitting, I could throw them as far as need be, with a heavy trout line and my eleven-foot Houghton rod. (The spear in the butt allows it to be used double-handed.) Some boldness in wading was needed, especially with an unkind wind, to get near enough to the fish. That too was part of the adventure. I had waders specially made which almost reached my neck. Only recently have I learned that some called me 'the otter' – from a distance they would not see much of me but my (then black-haired) head. I used to fish some fly casts which I have seen no-one else attempt.

At the bottom of Upper Ballathie, Colonel S. J. L. Hardie, a keen fly fisher, had built for himself a long casting platform slanting out to the edge of a deep channel down which most of the Tay pours. He defeated his purpose, as his side of the stream became too fierce for fly fishing, unless in *very* low water. He created thereby what may have been making him turn in his grave – a slaughter-house where sportsmen, sometimes seated on stools, kill fish after fish on large prawns usually dyed purple and suspended by large floats, or on bunches of worms sunk with gobbets of lead. But fished from the other side, the top of that fierce stream is ideal in low water with a little Logie or Blue Charm. One does not need to mend the line, since the current spontaneously swings the fly at the right speed over the quieter side of the current, where the fish lie at ease. The snag is that to reach it you have to wade across seventy-five yards of up-and-down bouldery water. Hooking fish there is much easier than landing them. Even if they oblige by going downstream to wear themselves out in the deeper water, you still have to coax them back through all those

* For about twenty-five years, I had written it 'ALDRENS' which is how locals pronounce it. I have changed my spelling, since noticing that the trees which fringe the stream are Alders.

boulders, which are sometimes weeded. In such situations a dropper fly is a menace. I did not expect to land more than one in three of the salmon I hooked in that corner.

In 1955 I left Dundee. Its University College was then part of St. Andrews University. Since the former was founded, there had been friction. It reached its climax during my eight years there. Despite my affection for St. Andrews I felt obliged to put the Dundee viewpoint to a series of enquiries which culminated with Lord Tedder's Royal Commission. The authorities in St. Andrews proposed to close the Dundee Arts departments, and substitute courses in Commerce (selling jute, etc.). The Royal Commission endorsed the compromise which I had advocated – that the Dundee College should have a Faculty of Social Science within which relevant Arts departments could flourish; and it also recommended that there should, for a start, be Professors of Economics, History and Philosophy. The Dundee dons who had criticised the St. Andrews proposals wished to preserve the union with St. Andrews and opposed civic demands for an independent university. (This later came into being.) We were not rewarded for our moderation, rather the opposite. Those of us who were able to escape did so. The Chair at Bangor fell vacant that summer. As things turned out I was very lucky to get it. At the time I was desolated at the prospect of leaving Tayside, its kindly folk, its salmonidae, the wild geese which flew over my home, etc. But no summers have passed without at least a week spent catching salmon on Stobhall or Cargill.

The Tay has been vaunted in verse. Scott opened *The Fair Maid of Perth* with this anonymous stanza:

> "Behold the Tiber!" the vain Roman cried,
> Viewing the ample Tay from Baiglie's side;
> "But where's the Scot that would the vaunt repay,
> And hail the puny Tiber for the Tay?"

And Dundee's eccentric bard MacGonagall wrote rhymes about 'the silvery Tay'. Yet, although it is Europe's most prolific salmon river, few anglers have sung its praises, at least in print. The Tay has spawned some classics, notably that of P. D. Malloch, but these concern the pioneering experiments from which so much was learned about the salmon's life history. As for the fishing, no-one has done for the Tay what Scrope did for the Tweed, Greene for the Bourne, Hutton for the Wye, etc. Grimble had to devote to the Tay one of his seventy-five chapters on Scottish rivers, and not all of his information about it is second-hand. He had no need to be reticent since he was, it seems, welcome on every salmon river in these islands. I have just found a short but handsome tribute to the fighting power of Tay salmon, tucked away in an autobiography by J. G. Millais. Much more is called for, however, and to try to redress the balance, I shall later give to the Tay some further overdue accolades.

North Wales

I knew Snowdonia only from a few climbing expeditions. My mother was sired by a Williams wed to a Parry, both of North Wales, so I should not have felt an alien; but at first I did. I spoke no Welsh. My colleagues were most hospitable, especially the Welsh-speakers. But like most mountain people, North-Walians are somewhat reserved, and after centuries of 'anglicisation' naturally tend to be somewhat suspicious of strangers. It took time to make friends, but I came to love the land of their fathers, and to appreciate their warm hearts and courtesy. I learned to see lowland Scots 'as ithers see us', a bit too impatient and 'pushing' by Welsh standards.

I was dismayed when first I peered from a bridge at the local 'salmon river'. I dismissed it as a mere burn and decided to concentrate on the Conway. Fortunately, however, I lost no time in getting my name on the waiting list for the Ogwen Fishing Club. I joined the Llanrwst Association, for the use of a few over-fished Conway pools. Some, presumably the best, were reserved for the villagers. The rest of the river was controlled by the Gwydyr Hotel at Betws-y-Coed, and day tickets on a limited stretch were available. 1956 was a good year for salmon on the Conway. The river was starting to reap the fruits of the pioneering work of Herbert Evans, the Fisheries Superintendent. He had cleared a small mountain lake of trout, and released a lot of salmon alevin therein. With the help of Dr. W. E. Jones of Liverpool University, he established that the survival rate was dramatically higher than in rivers, and that the time taken to reach the smolt stage was reduced on average by a year. The Conway was the first to benefit from these experiments. Later the method was used to increase the runs in most of the rivers of Snowdonia.

I enjoyed beginner's luck on the Conway. A flying visit between morning lectures and a 5 p.m. meeting produced a sea-liced fish, despite blazing sunshine, in the few yards of ripply water on the Llanrwst stretch. My first ticket day, in the first flood of May, yielded a salmon to a big fly in the Fir Tree Pool. Disillusionment soon set in. Once it was known that the fish were up, one had to queue to fish any pool worth fishing, and all the other anglers were using shrimps, mostly on floats. The Conway was once a fine fly river. It could be again. As others can confirm, incessant bombardment by shrimps (as well as by prawns) makes salmon well-nigh uncatchable on fly, unless you meet newcomers in a falling flood. Until he bought Dess in 1970, my friend Harry Calvert was a one-river man, perforce the Conway. He decided that if you can't beat them, join them, and he became a master of all forms of fishing the shrimp. But I quit, for I had, I found, a choice.

I had seen the shoals of salmon and seatrout in some of Ogwen's pools. It had been scorned unjustly. For its size, it was prolific, especially for seatrout. In the late 1950s it was yielding annually two to four hundred salmon to the rod and no-one knows how many seatrout. The River Board statistics were somewhat fictional – some of the most successful anglers were not in the habit of divulging their catches. And its bailiffs were never seen on the water of the more 'select' club.

I had to wait three years before election to this limited membership club. I was previously permitted a few days in Penrhyn Park, where my second visit yielded an eleven-pound seatrout. (Beginner's luck – it remained my biggest Ogwen seatrout.) My real apprenticeship on the Ogwen was in the unlimited membership club, which had most of the higher reaches. We fished cheek by jowl during summer floods. But the small run of salmon in early May did not seem to be common knowledge, and before my apprenticeship ended, it had become my custom after the first freshet in May to catch a brace, in solitude, on the lowest of the holding pools. I was disappointed, however, that they had to be caught on a spinning rod. I did spend a lot of time learning that fly fishing was unprofitable. In twenty-one years I got from the Ogwen only about a dozen on fly, and only one of them was on a little Low Water hook. One or two elderly anglers still tried a big fly, occasionally. There were very few pools, as distinct from boulder-strewn pockets overhung with oak trees, where a fly could be presented properly over a lie; and only a few hours, as raging torrent subsided to burn level, when the fish responded.

I had to learn a new form of spinning, sufficient of an art to be interesting. The proportion of offers missed and fish lost was appallingly high, by me initially, as well as by others. In big river downstream spinning, salmon hook themselves with the help of water pressure on the lure and the line. Down-stream spinning on these tiny pools proved most inefficient, unless in high floods, for the fish had time to grab and spit it out. The remedy I learned from a bailiff who spent most of his time fishing (and was soon to be sacked for snatching!) – up-stream spinning. It was exciting in clear water, as a fish left its lie and, often in full view, followed the devon down, and seized it in the act of turning up-stream – if it did not follow the lure so far that it saw you crouching. It demanded precision of casting from as far as possible below the lie, dropping the light-weight devon just where you could then bring it down, close to the fish and not too far from the river bed. The ratio of offers to fish landed improved dramatically.

At last my three years' apprenticeship ended. Long before then, I had fish-watched every pool of the two miles above the park, and *thought* that I knew every low water lie. It was a freak season. I got the two miles to myself (apart from the numerous poachers). The other twenty-three members went on waiting for the flood which never came. The River Board recorded a rod-catch of thirty-six for the whole river. I caught (and reported) thirteen of them. No floods came before the season ended, but a few freshets did. A three-inch rise was enough to tempt from the deep pools in the park the few fish which had not been destroyed there by the poachers' uses of lime, gelignite, etc. – activities not mentioned in the annual river reports. Unemployed slate-miners are as resourceful as the bombers of Brechin. There, I am told, a poacher who has blown off *both* his arms is relegated to the job of watching out for the bailiff.

From April to July, I did not miss a freshet. When asked what I had caught, I reported my tally. I had yet to learn that it was not the convention for successful anglers to blurt out the *whole* truth. I heard in due course that dark stories were circulating about my nefarious methods. But that season, at least, I obeyed all of the club rules, crazy though some of them were, notably that fishing must stop two hours after sunset – about the time that you should be starting to fish for the *very* shy Welsh 'sewin'.

At my first AGM I proposed the deletion of this rule. I was ruled out of order on the ground that the estate would certainly permit no changes in our rules. It was tactless for a newcomer to persist but still I tried to prompt some discussion. After the meeting I was advised by some senior members that this rule had for long been a dead letter and that I should fish, like them, as late as seatrout were in the mood. My raising of this issue led, however, to a deal of trouble. The inconsistency between rule and practice was at last resolved a decade later. Then we found to our relief that the estate did not regard the antique rules as sacrosanct. When the point was at last conveyed, it was readily taken – that it was better to have some honest anglers fishing in the dark than to issue an open invitation to those who used gelignite, nets and poisons.

The virtues of the Ogwen, for me at least, included the fact that very few salmon or seatrout ran (to tempt me) until I had finished teaching and examining. Another was that floods produced salmon, and dry spells first-class seatrout fishing (for the rule breakers). Not that I often fished on the day of a big flood, when everyone else was out worming. The day that followed was when I caught salmon. It took only three or four hours to fish known lies, if one wasted no time elsewhere. Then, if no rain returned, on the evening of the next day the new run of seatrout would be settled and ready for the fly. Apart from my first fanatical season, I fished the Ogwen regularly throughout July before leaving for the Tay, so I got very few of the finnock which ran thereafter. July was the month for the bigger seatrout, and few seasons passed without some of five pounds or more, and an average weight close to two pounds. I am sure that I was never top scorer, apart from the first year. Though he did not disclose his tally, my friend Mac must always have been well in the lead for both salmon and seatrout. He had fished the water for many decades and when I had got to know him, he was generous in passing on some of his knowledge.

I have caught salmon and seatrout in several other Snowdonian streams, but the Ogwen is my love. From Bethesda to the sea it is the prettiest little river that I know. Some of the native oaks have now been hewn for the inevitable conifer plantations, but many remain, and with them red squirrels. One meets an occasional otter or kingfisher. Buzzards sometimes soar above. I knew it at its best. It now seems to be well on its way to destruction. A large firm took over the slate quarry about ten years ago, and introduced machinery which produces vast quantities of slate dust. This they released from late afternoon, so that the river became full of the gray brew, which sickens the fish, before seatrout time.

The meandering miles in the Nant Ffrancon Pass have been made into a straight canal by the River Board, drainage to nourish a few more sheep, and as a result of the more sudden and violent floods the best of the seatrout pools, built nearly 100 years ago with cobbled weirs, are silted up and useless, and some of the pools on whose construction our Club spent its savings are destroyed. The seatrout have dwindled in size and in numbers, as elsewhere in the country, presumably due to the many poisons which men send to sea. The runs of salmon have still not fully recovered from the cyanide poisoning in August of 1969, when 260 fresh-run salmon were collected dead. I was lucky to know it in its fishing prime.

Eire

Ireland being so accessible from Bangor, I decided to seek pastures new for spring fishing. Having read Mrs. N. K. Robertson's charming book *Thrifty Salmon Fishing*, I wrote to her. Happily for me, one of her party of fishing (paying) guests had called off and the three others agreed to risk having a stranger in their midst. Mrs. Robertson proved to be as witty a hostess as she was a writer, a racy raconteuse when she presided at our breakfast and dinner table. We each fished separate beats, and these rotated. Flood and mud made the River Slaney unfishable for the first two days. On Wednesday I was driven to the top of the top beat, two miles above the hut.

The water was now clear enough for spinning and my spirits rose. But at the first cast I got stuck on the bottom and in my impatience to get going I broke my spinning rod at the ferrule. Rather than waste an hour or two seeking a substitute, I removed the end ring and taped it nine inches beyond the large ring on the butt. It was atrocious to handle, but I could still get a big devon across most of the river. I played a fish but the hook tore out, not surprisingly. I decided that if opportunity knocked again, I must, contrary to my custom, loosen the reel's slipping clutch. Opportunity did knock. The party was encouraged at lunch to see the first fish of the week, and more than surprised by the stump with which it had been caught. The joke was that before the accident halved the length of my rod, it measured only seven feet; and in her book Mrs. Robertson had made dismissive cracks about such 'toothpick rods'. She lent me one which met with her approval.

Saturday was the red-letter day. We all had sport – eleven fish, all but one on fly. I was very lucky to land my first which anchored my dropper on a rock. When I finally decided to break, it was the moss and not the cast which gave. Having got a second on fly that morning, I invited Mrs. Robertson to share my rod that afternoon. We took alternate pools. She cast a bonny line and got a fish on a fly of her own tying. I took my second lesson from Fitz, the ghillie, in worm fishing. In lesson one, I had done all that he told me – let a fish take the worms back to its lie, given it time to start chewing, and struck on command. The hook which came back was the bluntest hook I ever felt! Poor Fitz – it was his hook. Lesson two was successful in the first pool that I fished. My prejudice against worming was reduced. It was really quite exciting trying to decide how long to wait before striking.

My hope that I had started an annual event was to be disappointed – the upkeep of Clonegal Castle obliged Mrs. Robertson next year to

Where the author caught his first Spey seatrout in solitude. *Arthur Oglesby*

Harry concentrating on Kincardine water.

Potarch pool on the Borrowstone beat.

Mid-Dee in May-time. *Arthur Oglesby*

The fishing pools of the Morar. Above: The top of the Island Pool.

Below: The tail of the Broad Pool viewed from that grassy verge.

let three-quarters of the water for the season. She kindly let me have a week on what remained. I landed four weighing fifty-two pounds, unfortunately all on a spinning rod. Next year, I decided that I must reconnoitre for a place to combine spring fishing with a holiday for my family. Sheila and I drove around the West of Eire without success until we reached Bundoran Hotel. The owner offered me a day on the River Drowes if I stayed until Saturday. For the first time I agreed to employ a ghillie. A beginner would not know where to start in the flat and featureless lower water to which I expected to be allocated. I was glad that I did.

Pat was a keen angler and a good teacher. He taught me three ways to fish 'the shrimp' (really a baby prawn), which he impaled on a single round hook and secured with thin pink rubber. He used them as flies (gently cast), dangled from a cork, and by sink and draw, all with a fly rod. I started the day using fly and invited him to follow me down with a shrimp. After he had caught a fish and lost another, I succumbed: 'O.K. Show me how'. The up-stream wind had increased. This suits the cork method, he said, as the waves keep the shrimp bobbing up and down. Several times my cork dipped momentarily. I had to be warned not to strike too soon, as this indicated a fish nosing the bait. At last it went down with aplomb and the fish was firmly hooked. Another method acquired for the days when flies were ignored!

When I paid my bill on Sunday morning, my host said: 'You might be interested in Lareen Lodge'. It emerged that he let this Lodge for £30 per calendar month, with a rod on the river and a boat on Loch Melvyn thrown in. It seemed too good to be true. Sheila was persuaded to drive there and have a look. The 'Lodge' was a small cottage by the ruins of the original Lodge, but the site was a dream. Blazing with daffodils from the trees to the river bank, and two real salmon pools within a stone's throw. Between them, and up to the exit of Lough Melvyn, large trout were feasting on flies. Paradise! We had to catch the afternoon boat at Dun Laoghaire, and had no time to go back to plead for next April's tenancy. My beseeching letters pulled it off, however, and for the next three years, we were the April tenants.

The angling advantages were greater than could have been anticipated. Has any other hotel weighted the scales so much in favour of a *non*-resident? The residents were alloted beats, most of them on the miles of boring flats. The mile from the 'Lodge' down was one beat, with salmon pools alternating with trouty shallows all the way. The Lareen tenant, fortunately lacking a telephone, was free to fish anywhere on the river!

In due course, I booked Pat for the odd day when he was free, and he showed me the lies in the bottom half-mile where some of the fish which escape the trap below the estuary bridge tarry for a while. I caught among others a twenty-four-pounder in a place where I should not have considered fishing; for one had to hurl a shrimp over a thick reed-bed and let it swim down below the opposite bank. I picked up the local method of fishing fly in dead water – pulling it in short jerks just below the surface. I later practised this method with more success on some deep dark pools above Llanrwst. It did not get me many fish on the River Drowes, but when it did it was a thrill to see the salmon ascending from the brown depths, while curbing the impulse to strike. This impulse reasserts itself when one keeps oscillating between trout and salmon fishing; and I hated missing the trouts' midday rise – most of them being succulent gillaroos not yet back in the lough after spawning in the river.

An odd coincidence occurred during my second to last spring at Lareen. That was my only April when the river seemed to be empty of salmon, other than kelts. The many fish which had run in March had apparently reached Lough Melvyn. I was due to depart on the 21st of the month. I had fished for two weeks without seeing a fresh salmon. The patience of our au pair girl was wearing thin, like mine. She had been looking forward to eating the promised salmon. On the morning of the 16th she announced at breakfast: 'Today you will catch a salmon. I saw it happening clearly in a dream.' Could she, I asked, identify the pool? 'Oh yes', she said, 'you were standing on the island.' I took this with a large grain of salt. Of course she would picture it happening on the Island Pool, visible from the kitchen window and only 100 yards below the cottage. I had had a quick cast there every day of each visit but never with success.

That day I fished for trout in the morning. Then after lunch, I started with a salmon fly at the top of the little island. Within a minute a salmon came up aggressively at my fly – but did not touch it. Another kelt? It rose in a leisurely manner to inspect each of the next two flies which I showed it. I then tried with a shrimp fly, a local favourite, and at last it took with a bang. My son who was watching called her from the cottage and the dreamer came down to witness the landing of that fish which was *not* a kelt. Precognition? It was, at least, surprising. Thereafter I fished the Island Pool assiduously. I caught two more salmon that April, and got back into double figures the following spring. Yet in the Island Pool I did not receive a second offer.

I would gladly have spent a lifetime of spring holidays at Lareen, but alas the family grew restless. After three springs, all of the local walks and expeditions had been done many times over. My son had caught a few gillaroos with glee, but it didn't take. He evinced no urge to catch more. The little cottage was a coop for the others when it rained. For the greater good of the greater number, I let it lapse.

Less fortunate forays

So far my memory has been wearing rose-coloured spectacles. It has not all been undiluted joy and success – especially in spring when seeking salmon. After losing Lareen, I had to wait for eight years before I was again to admire my springers on daffodilled banks. By Falkus's yardstick my next spring foray was not a failure; the week yielded eight weighing eighty-four pounds, with four on the last day. But it wasn't *fun*. I was sampling Ireland's Tay, the Cork Blackwater, on the Lower Kilbarry stretch. A lot of water, but only two of the pools would gladden the eye of an angler who had been spoilt. According to the thermometer, they should have been taking the flies, which I cast for half the week without an offer. The water, though clear, was apparently too high. I resigned myself to offering what the fish wanted – 1¾ in. devons. I am glad, for her sake, that I did not bring Sheila: she would have hated the barn-like hotel. I spent lonely evenings supping Guinness with no conversation. I had picked a hotel not frequented by anglers, and had forgotten to bring some light reading.

With much misgiving, I returned to the same water next April, and it was a failure by all possible standards. I saw only one coloured fish which leapt regularly out of range. After four days of flogging I knew it was hopeless. They were catching nothing on the up-stream beat where, below a weir, retired Prime Ministers, etc., normally get their daily dozen. For the first time in my life, I abandoned fishing which I had paid for; to see Kerry, but in weather as gloomy as my own mood.

Departing briefly from gloom (and chronological order), let me add that my happiest holiday in Eire was several years later – a few days with Sheila at the end of May, seeing the sights of Cork and Kerry. To keep Satan behind my back, the only tackle I put in the car was a trout rod and a few flies. (Sheila has had an overdose of rivers and lochs. She spent her childhood holidays, she says, waiting for her father to have 'the last cast', on banks or in boats, in rain and/or gale). Perhaps kissing the Blarney stone blessed our trip. We revelled in the scenery. The huge hawthorns in bloom do for Eire what cherries must do for Japan. Only once, I think, did I strain Sheila's patience by spending too long catching small trout. I would keep only enough of them to fry at our midday picnics. I did disgrace myself during my two hours on Lake Killarney. The evening rise was slow to start, but when it came I was broken by fish after fish. I was experimenting that holiday with *very* light nylon casts – ideal for little loughs in bright sunshine, but I never used it again. I could read the boatman's caustic thoughts as he silently rowed this duffer ashore. But it didn't matter. I met an evening rise on a more remote lake next evening.

Now back to the gloom. A trip to the Wye, of which I had read so much; to catch my first *English* salmon. (I still have not done so.) I bet Arthur Hutton never fished that hotel's stretch. The hotel was very nice, but its water! It must have held good pike, but I never saw a salmon, or even a rising trout. Again I quit before the end of my week.

Then there was that frustrating week at Aberlour. Lots of lovely shallow streams, ideal for the summer salmon. If there was a holding pool, I failed to find it. Drought level, glacial water and bright sun could not have helped less. Yet gentlemen with Rolls-Royces returned each evening to display in the hotel lobby fish caught in deep pools down-stream. I stuck it out till 4 p.m. on Saturday. At any rate the others on the hotel water were likewise fishless. As I engaged first gear, I glanced back towards the pool which I had just fished – to see a beginner bouncing around with a bending rod. He got back late with two good fish. With the help of a dram, I managed to share his pleasure. Unfairly, no doubt, I have grown suspicious of free, or cheap, hotel water.

When Harry acquired Dess and a mile of the Dee, I dropped a heavy hint: if you need any help with those salmon . . . I arrived next April and was knocked out by the stateliness of his new home, and the glorious views from the house and garden. There, through a niche in the trees was Lochnagar, whose summit Sheila and I had reached while courting. But spring had not yet touched Deeside. The water was shrunken by frost and the air remained close to freezing point. Harry's angling report was bleak. He is the most efficient and indefatigable sportsman I know. Yet his efforts since February had yielded only one fish – as a guest elsewhere.

It was the upper mile of Dess water which he now owned. It turned out later to be splendid summer water, fast shallow streams loved by fish short of oxygen. From charity to Harry, landed with a guest, his neighbour, Brigadier Bradford, had generously offered us the use of his Kincardine stretch for the second half of the week. We started with hope, if not confidence, as we knew that there were fish around – a shoal lay comatose below Aboyne Bridge. We were not discouraged by three blank days on Dess, for we had seen a few, including a twenty-pounder which jumped almost over my rod when I was wading (too) deep. Kincardine has several first-class holding pools for springers. Well, we saw one or two in the Calm Pool, but that was all. Not a kelt, not an offer. My heart bled for Harry. I tried not to show it. Unlike us Celts, he is not one for wearing his heart on his sleeve. We diverted ourselves with some evening pigeon-shooting. On Saturday evening he said, casually, 'I don't suppose you'll want to come back?' My answer was 'Try me. Do you think I'll willingly be beaten by the Dee?'

Perhaps he feared that I had not enjoyed it. I had loved every minute. Quite apart from his company and lavish hospitality, I really enjoyed the fishing; because I was fishing with hope and indeed expectation. So far as I am concerned, Falkus got it wrong. According to his confident assertions, I suffered from 'a strange form of self-deception' in thinking that I enjoyed that week. He wrote:

> 'Was there ever a game fisher yet who by the end of a fishless week gave a damn about the birds and the flowers, or the view or anything else? His sense of deep inner contentment comes from one thing only – the sight of a fish on the bank. If such a person as a happy unsuccessful game fisherman exists I can only say that I have never met him' (1st ed., p. 156).

Well, I should like to meet Mr. Falkus, if only to find if his lust for fish *really* annihilates the love of nature which seems so manifest in his other works.

Some anglers boast of their unsuccessful pottering. Andrew Lang wrote: 'Some men are born duffers. Others, unlike persons of genius, become so by an infinite capacity for not taking pains'; and he claimed to belong to both these classes. However, like Falkus, and Harry, when there is a chance of a fish, I am no potterer. It would be humbug to say that I enjoy fishing *as much* when my score has been nought. For me, the difference between one salmon and none is greater than that between one and ten. But a blank does not spoil my day, so long as I have fished, *expecting* a fish. When hope dies, one becomes a machine and the mind demands other occupations. Admittedly, hope dies more quickly on unfamiliar waters. I could never fish at Stobhall, for example, without much more than hope. Memories of past encounters would fuel my anticipation even if, inconceivably, I suffered there a decade of blank days. In the case of the Dee, my confidence was fuelled by the writings of (or about) Wood of Cairnton, Crossley, Waddington and others. Thank goodness Harry did not just take it for granted that I would not wish to return. I became a regular visitor in the first week of April.

The Royal Dee

Next April the Dee redeemed itself, though I missed my hosts' company – they were skiing. So I had the use of Dess House and the Landrover, the help of the housekeeper and if need be, the keeper, and the choice of fishing Dess or, as recommended, the rod that Harry had now rented on Kincardine, or occasionally Borrowstone, the beat below. Clearly I had a moral obligation to catch some fish. Happily was it fulfilled. I got seven, and what most gratified my vanity was catching the first (four) to be taken on fly in that part of the river. I nearly fell in with excitement when I hooked the first on a No. 4 Hairy Mary, wading down the Village Pool.

What surprised me most about the local salmon fishing, as confirmed by the Dess records covering about a century, was that fly fishing started on, or a week or so earlier than, 15 April; the date from which spinning was now banned, except in floods. Had the habits of Dee salmon altered since Wood stopped fishing in 1934, or do their habits change while travelling a few miles up from Cairnton? I found both alternatives hard to believe. Between 1913 and 1934 Wood had caught 3,490 salmon, all, I think, on fly; and according to 'Jock Scott', Wood recorded in 1934 that 'forty-three per cent of my fish caught in February in the last ten years were taken on the greased line and small fly, sixty-five per cent in March, ninety-four per cent in April'. Had the news not travelled up-stream? The disease known as Ulcerative Dermal Necrosis (UDN) does seem to stop fish from taking flies (or anything else), but in 1970 and 1971 I saw no sign of this disease, which was to take a heavy toll in the ensuing years.

I set out to verify whether Wood's techniques still worked, with some, though limited, success. On arriving at Dess, my first question has always been 'Any yet on fly?'; hoping for a 'No', and the chance to be the first. Sometimes I have been, and once I had a near miss. That was in 1972 after an event which had already made my week. At a pause for tea near the summit of Cairn o'Mount, an *eagle owl* nearly knocked me down as I stood stock-still in the heather. I had watched its approach for a mile as it flew across the empty, sombre moorland, hunting and occasionally stooping. I dropped my binoculars when it filled my visual field. We were equally startled. I by its wingspan of five or six feet. Its surprise was clear from the what-the-hell-are-you-doing-here look in its glaring orange eyes. It did not change course and I felt the draught from its wings. No bird men believed me, of course, since I am not an Accredited Ornithologist; and one very recent bird book says that no eagle owls have been sighted in the UK this century. They are unmistakable, even asleep in London Zoo.

To return to my near miss. It was spinning water all week. By 5 p.m. on my second to last day, I was resigned to failure with the fly. As I drank my tea, meditating whether to save my energy for Saturday, a certain fish showed again. It had displayed itself hourly all day – a fat, fresh fifteen pounder, in a lie easily covered from the bank. I had already showed to it flies of sizes four and six. Now, noticing that the cold wind had abated, I decided to give it one more chance. I chose a number 1 Jock Scott. Unfortunately, it had but a single hook. I fancied a large Jock but I had none dressed on a double hook.

This salmon lay in fast water and the fly swam just below the surface, for the fish came up like a dolphin, slewing sideways and out-stream as it went down. It fought a magnificent battle. For nearly twenty minutes it made full use of the weight of the current, and seemed as strong as Harry. My heart stuck in my mouth. Knowing that there is a fifty per cent chance of a large single fly hook losing its hold, I dared not pull too hard. Finally I got the fish within a few yards of the only foot of grass where it could be beached. Three times it turned on its side on the surface and let me draw it from the edge of the strong current. Twice it mustered the strength to wriggle back. The third time I said 'Time up'. The fly was visibly in the corner of its mouth, the hook was surely in the scissors, the hold would surely survive a few more seconds of firm strain. It didn't. I gripped line against rod with my left hand, and the fly flew back at me. My beautiful fish slowly sank and drifted down-stream.

Such was my disappointment that I cast myself on the bank, to mourn my errors – jumping to the conclusion that the fish was hooked in the scissors, not the tongue – taking hold of the line; and *especially* forgetting my gaff. I had always carried a telescopic gaff when salmon fishing in the spring. For three years I had found no use for it, except as a priest. But until very recently I had, when preparing to beach a fish, opened the gaff and kept it under my left arm or on the ground, ready for just this situation – an exhausted fish which comes unstuck at the last gasp. I would not forget again. Fortunately such sorrows do not last for long. One remembers Walton's consoling words: 'No man can lose what he never had'. Next morning Mrs. Bradford caught one on fly and I sent my congratulations.

Deeside in early April can provide a vast variety of weather. In 1974 I sweltered in shirt-sleeves. The water shot up from thirty-eight to fifty-four degrees – too fast for the fish, it seemed, as I nearly had a blank week. In 1975, I drove up through the spring blizzard of the decade (century?) and fortunately funked the road over Cairn o'Mount. Much of Deeside including Dess was without electricity for two days. By tea-time on Tuesday, the snow blew less thickly and visibility was up to 100 yards. I ventured out and tried a cast on Kincardine and the third produced a fish. After twenty minutes my hands were unusable blocks of ice. Harry went down with skiing gloves and was soon back with a second.

Next morning, a hot sun filled the river with small icebergs, 'grue'. They had just melted by 12.30, but the sun now shone down-stream. I waited at the ready for that tiny cloud to cross the sun, then tempted the twenty-pounder which had recently started to show. Harry arrived in time to help me beach it, having come to find if it was yet worthwhile fishing. I remember that week also as the only occasion when I got running fish in the middle of a day of rapidly rising water; and Harry did too. We tied with eight each that week, good fish, despite the way it started.

I hope a chance may come for further experiment. I want to find if it is really true (as I have been told) that Wood's success with the floating line in February and March was because the Cairnton beat was then stacked with fish which made it their first stop in fresh water. To be fair, the experiment must follow Wood to the letter. In the Kincardine region, when a fly is first tried, it is not what Wood prescribed, namely a No. 1 Low Water Single, but a dumpy double-hook, sized six or eight, or a medium-large heavy single iron. Wood-style No. 1s are long hooks, though very short on the dressing. I know that when Mallochs accidentally included two of these among the doubles I had ordered, the use of one on the dropper got a Dee salmon and two more offers in the last hour of the week, before I broke it at dusk on a stone.

Of course, there are many spring days when it would be daft to fish with fly. And if one has to spin on the Dee, one had better use the most effective ironmongery: the huge spoons made by Willie Blair of Kincardine, the fat, not the thin, model. And persuade him, as I did, to add a second hook half-way down, for the fish which take the spoon broadside on. Harry improved my prototype by using a double hook, instead of a treble, for the middle position; and he has had the chance to prove the attractions of these spoons for salmon not spawned in the Dee. And when it is hopeless even with these spoons, you can cheer yourself up by a visit to Willie. He loves to talk about fishing, is by nature a philosopher, and you will come away with hope renewed. In any case, you can enjoy 'the most beautiful sight anyone can see'. This description of the scenery is that of Frederick Hill. He had twenty years to gaze at it, looking across at Dess and Kincardine from the banks of Carlogie.

2
Ask And It Shall Be Given Unto You

I suppose I was lucky not to have lived a generation later. In the last two decades, fishing, especially for salmon and seatrout, has become so commercialised and expensive. With help of pollution, water abstraction and other forms of destruction, Nature's resources have been getting over-strained. The number of silver salmonidae which return to their birth-places has progressively dwindled in many rivers. I am sure that young men would now find it much more difficult than Jim and I did to gain the privilege simply by asking, of fishing some of Scotland's finest waters.

Perhaps it helped that we made it clear that our families had eaten a surfeit of our catches, and sought only the pleasure of landing some for their lawful owners. It may also have helped that we sometimes donned the kilt when, as strangers, we knocked at the door of a riparian owner. For us, at least, the direct approach worked wonders, and I shall describe some of its fruits. It should not be inferred that we were interested only in scrounging free fishing. Nearly all the angling to be described in this section could not have been bought. Of course, we willingly paid for our fishing elsewhere, and sometimes also on the Tay; for then one could lease the odd day even during the peaks of the spring and autumn runs.

On the Spey near Carrbridge

According to the books, the Grantown stretch is the top of the Spey's salmon fishing water. I can understand why the books ignore, despite their nice names, tributaries like the Truim and the Tromie, since their output, if rod-caught, is caught by the worm in the floods of late summer and autumn. It must, however, be due to ignorance that they fail to mention a certain marvellous mile, tucked away between so much pike water.

When I distributed at Carrbridge some of my first two salmon, someone suggested that I approach Major Dunbar who lived on the far bank of the river. I did not act on this until the following spring. I found a dear old gentleman, too frail to walk further than the seat by his nearest pool, but happy to talk of the past. I was welcomed to try for a fish, though he thought it was really too early. It wasn't quite. I got one clean fish on a spinner among the plethora of kelts. But I snatched two days at the end of May, and they produced two successes – that dawn fish (p. 14) and one caught by my mother-in-law to be described later (p. 58). For the next four years, I became a regular guest – for a week in early April and a few days at the end of May.

I shall describe one dazzling morning of the next May. When fly fishing if the sun shone, its direction confined one to the mornings. (Blessed are they whose rivers run from north to south.) That morning was the first time for me that everything went *à la* Wood, for several fish. In early sunshine I first beheld, at summer level, the series of rocky, rushing, pools below the Major's house. I started at 7 a.m. in the likeliest looking of them, with Logies, a No. 6 on the tail and a No. 8 on the dropper. Not yet very wide awake, I had a boil *and struck*, trout style. As Chalmers has said, this is as reprehensible as striking a woman. The No. 8 remained in the fish's jaw. Kicking myself, I replaced the tail fly with a No. 8 and did not tarry to replace the dropper. I had not long to wait.

In the strong water near the tail of the pool a fish took hold on a taut line, and the fight was on. It was an anxious and cautious fight, for I knew that it could not be hooked *à la* Wood (i.e. in the scissors), and I could not forget that the hook was *very* small. That fish embarrassed me in the later stages by running up between my legs and proceeding for some distance up my wading water. Thank goodness I had no dropper fly. Had there been a spectator, I should have looked absurd. I was facing down-stream, with my twelve-foot rod bent double. The line was rubbing the crutch of my waders, and I was peering over my shoulder trying to keep an eye on the fish. Fortunately it was well-hooked, and it paused while I did my awkward balancing act and lifted one leg underwater over the tight line. The gleaming twelve-pounder was then ready to be lifted out by the tail.

The fishable part of the pool above was a smooth but pacy glide. Its inhabitants seemed, like me, to have studied Wood. For the first time I had that surprising experience which he describes. A certain fish repeatedly boiled at the fly two or three times as it came round, but without touching it. I spent a lot of time changing to different sizes and patterns until it was, I thought, 'put down' for the day. It was only when I resumed at last, after a short rest, with the Logie No. 8 that this teaser took hold. We had an exciting tussle but the hold gave when the fish was at last near a beaching place. What recked it, since the birds sang, the sun was warm, and there was lots of time for another? Near the tail of the same pool, the same drama repeated itself. This little hook was *not* finding its proper home in the scissors.

This was, however, my own fault. I was not following in the Master's footsteps in one respect which he deemed essential: holding two yards of loose line to give away when a fish took hold; so that a belly of line would form and pull the fly home from the side or from down below. When, in later years, I tried to master this technique I never really succeeded. Sometimes it worked, but not consistently; for sometimes my left hand's fingers would instinctively tighten before I let go, only momentarily, but apparently for long enough to prick the fish and make it let go. Such lapses were what led me to have my flies, at least for the tail position, dressed on Low Water *double*-hooks. These I have found, over the years, are highly efficient in hooking and holding salmon. With doubles (or trebles) you can leave a fish to hook itself, provided, of course, that your rod and line are not both pointing straight to your fly! You need to give a fish time to suck in your fly, and close its jaws, and turn, before it feels the pressure.

I have digressed again. The pool which produced a fish at 7 a.m. produced two more after its long rest. Not big, but beautiful fresh-run eight pounders; and with no more teasing or losses. The little Logie was worn out when the Major's man came down at 1 p.m. to see if I had a fish which he could take to the local hospital. Wood and Crossley had not exaggerated the joys of the greased-line method. I felt that I had graduated, as a *D.A*. and not a mere Fellow.

There were other such May mornings. One started on similar lines – with two early fish on a little Logie from the Major's home pools. About to work my way up-stream to other now familiar pools, I met, to my dismay, a man who had just fished all the way down *spinning* an enormous red prawn. He too was fishing for the Major, but so far without success. For what denizens of the deep, I wondered, can salmon mistake *revolving* prawns? I changed my plans and drove to the top pool where the fish might have recovered from their shock. It was then so bright and sultry and the quiet deep pool looked so dead that I felt no faith even in Logie.

I decided to take on my rival at his own game. I had among the junk in my car a package of Hardy's preserved prawns, unopened. I decided to fish them as they should, surely, be fished – sink and draw, moving in the way they jerk backwards in saline rock-pools. Making a mount is a moment's work, if you have at hand a needle, a sizeable triangle hook and some twenty-pound Alasticum wire.

The fish were, after all, prawn crazy. The river was very low and clear, and its surface unruffled. I started well above the main lie, which is just below a big boulder, with a trial cast to see how the prawn looked in the water. It had scarcely started its induced jerks when I saw, shooting up-stream from the boulder, a fish whose aim was bang on; and then fought like a tiger. The next cast was careless. It did not reach the middle of the river. But the prawn was barely in the water, when a bow wave came at it from near the far bank, and the red devil was seized again. Another manic salmon leapt all around the pool. I had proved my (private) point, and had caught enough to please the Major. I spent the rest of the morning verifying my hunch that it was too sultry for a fly, even Logie, to move a fish.

The Major died soon after I went into exile. I regret that this belated tribute to his kindness comes much too late for him to read.

In the region of Morar and Ailort

By 1953, it was clear that the interests of my wife and weans required summer holidays in some suitable place, preferably near to sea and sand. If we found one near to good fishing that would be a windfall for me. While 'Gran' looked after the weans, Sheila and I did an unarmed reconnaissance of the North-West coast. We fell for the silver sands of Morar, and spent about two days searching, from Arisaig to Mallaig, for a cottage not fully booked up. We had given up hope when someone said that she had heard a rumour that Mrs. Shaw-Stewart *might* start letting her Gate House. We hastened there. It looked ideal, about ten yards from the sands, far beyond which lay the Cuillins, and Rum and Eigg and Muck. For the next five years we were the very contented July tenants.

Appropriately, my fishing began modestly. It took a lot of asking before I found Mr. Macdonnell, a shepherd, who agreed to manage his boat while I fished Loch Morar. I was lucky to find a man so deft with his boat. Most of my eight good trout were due to his spotting one move in the two-foot waves and telling me where to cast, or, because the fish was too close, doing a quick quiet backward circle to give me the needed time and space; and to following his advice to use very large flies. However, the bit we both enjoyed most was being driven back, over white topped three-foot waves, by his outboard engine. Thank goodness it took the strain. I was remembering that day when Jim and I had been caught in a western gale at the east end of Loch Leven. It took three hours, with two of us pulling at each enormous oar. At the jetty we slumped on the oars, like the Blues do at the end of the Oxbridge boat-race. (*And* we were fishless.)

And then I heard that the Factor of Arisaig Estate let a privileged few have the odd day on 'the Mains Loch' (Loch nan Eila); and he granted me two days. When I first saw it, I wondered that it was called 'loch' not 'lochan'. Most of the large pond was occupied by water-lilies. Its virtue was due to its short and easy access from the sea. It was there that I learnt, in the small boat, to combine the arts of boatman and angler – almost continuously since, whichever way the wind blew, one had to weave between weed-patches. Incredibly, none of the many seatrout which I caught there had the sense to run into the weeds – they ran, leaped and bored in the scanty open water. They seemed, as Lord Grey put it, 'too chivalrous to take so great an advantage of the angler'.

I was well enough pleased with my first day – four weighing 5½ lb. As I later learnt, that was an off day. My second produced thirteen seatrout and three finnock. My best day there could have been much better, but for the pain in my jaw. A flood had just filled the little loch with seatrout. Fortunately I knew where the weed banks lay as many were still below water. By mid-afternoon, when I had twenty-nine seatrout, I gave in to the pain. Over four hours were wasted burning the miles to and from Fort William. I cursed myself all the way back. All that the dentist had done was to lance the enormous abscess. I could have done it with my penknife. I then spent two evening hours, trying to make it thirty; but the fish were off, perhaps off to the upper loch scared by a family of otters so absorbed in their games that they sometimes came within casting distance of the boat.

It was not always easy. If the sun blazed, one had to have a ripple. Moist south-west winds with a smirr of rain ('Scotch mist') proved most profitable – and such weather was too frequent on that western seaboard to please the rest of my family. My best fish there weighed 5½ lb. It took me by surprise on a hot bright afternoon, when I thought it was casting practice. The Factor too was surprised to hear that such fish entered the Mains Loch. This one was very unlucky to lose that long battle. The breeze kept drifting the boat near to the dense weeds which stretched along the east shore. I had to keep pulling alternative oars with my left hand. This made the light boat zigzag but produced little up-wind movement. My net seemed too small, so even when the fish had tired, it took about half an hour's labour to reach the small piece of the west bank which was clear of weeds. When the boat at last ground ashore the exhausted seatrout was easily beached.

Mrs. Shaw-Stewart enjoyed eating seatrout, and kindly introduced me to Mrs. Cameron-Head of Inverailort. She could not offer a day on Loch Eilt. Being one of the great dapping lochs, it was booked out by devotees who returned each season. Fortunately she retained half of the River Ailort, a rotating half. The tenant for the loch could also fish the river, but rarely did – one half in the morning, the other in the afternoon. A guest had the rest. To complete my bonus in that first July, I had two guest days on the Ailort. From what I later learnt, they were, in one sense, wasted – catching a lot of finnock and some one-pound seatrout. Having spent days at Bridge of Dun *not* catching *small* finnock while some experts succeeded, it was a new experience to find sizeable finnock so eager for my little Peter Ross. The first afternoon I did not need to budge from a pool below a little waterfall beneath the exit from Loch Eilt. Evidently the finnock were ascending continuously. Oh, to be there when the ten pounders were running; but they did that a month or two earlier in the year. In the pools near the sea, catching finnock was really too easy, and I kept only the best.

So far, apart from the Mains Loch, I have recalled only that first July. Better things were still to come. In my introduction to the Ailort, I had missed two potential places for big fish. Below the waterfall where I had my first success, lay the keeper's cottage and little Loch Dubh. It should have been called Loch Dour. For me at least it remained a mere potential, but very provoking. When some imperceptible barometrical change occurred, huge seatrout slapped about. After seeing this happen, I showed them annually, from boat and bank, innumerable flies; I waited for the witching hours – dusk to dark; I tried little heavy-weight devons so successful with Ythan seatrout. Apart from a few finnock, they gave me the cold shoulder – which spread large waves across the loch. I was told by someone that the way to catch them was to leave a worm on the gravel below the river's entry, but I never got desperate enough for that.

The other potential was fulfilled. It was a pool in the lower half, scoured deep by a huge boulder and a (relatively) long gravelly tail. One could see the salmon and seatrout by peeping over the big boulder, thereby making them do tight circles in the deep hole. I never explored all the pools, but none could have been better designed for dusk fishing, when, of course, the seatrout dropped back to the gravel bed. There I enjoyed several fast and furious sessions. Some were shared with Jim, and then we took turns in catching fish – there was room for, as well as a right to use, only one rod. Here at last I got two-pound Ailort seatrout. I had not envisaged catching salmon on seatrout flies in that tail. But this happened too, several times. They took quite a while to land with a nine foot rod. I can still smell the pungent bracken – and feel my midge smitten skin, which ceased to be anaesthetised as soon as the fish stopped taking.

The best is yet to come. Before it was got at by the Hydro-Electric Board, the River Morar was about four furlongs long, though the upper half was a useless flat. They built their dam in the top pool, then the best. This left two pools. (An angler would not count the one below the bridge as it goes up and down at high tides.) They devised a fish ladder which foxed the fish. Some of them must find it, but the task takes time. The result was that the two pools got *very* congested with fish. Rows of them extended in each of the three dimensions. (A query for biologists. We all know the hierarchical order adopted by a shoal of salmonidae, with the bigger fish up-stream. Is there also a pecking order in the vertical dimension with the biggest on the river bed?).

On the twenty days of that second July when I was not fishing, I was deep in sin – the sin of Envy. It must be as wicked to covet a neighbour's water, as his wife, or ox or ass. When passing by I stopped my car by the grassy verge above the Sea-Pool bridge. I never gazed for very long as the burden of sin got uncomfortable. 'Want what you have got or can get' is a good maxim, but a child may find it hard not to want the moon; as I wanted the Morar. This is one case when I did not ask, not out loud anyway. It would have been as brazen as asking the Queen for a rod at Balmoral. Angling Medical Professors had holidayed there for decades without seeking a day even on the Ailort, and I was a mere lecturer in an obscure subject. Mrs. Shaw-Stewart was perceptive as well as kind. I may have sighed, over that cup of tea, as I made a passing comment on those *lovely* pools. Anyway she got the message, and I do not think she needed second sight. She 'phoned Mrs. Stirling who owned the north bank. You could have knocked me down with a Logie 8, when she told me that evening that I was allotted the six hours from noon tomorrow.

The system involved each owner having, alternatively, the use of the whole river, both banks, both pools. At ten minutes before noon, my rod was at the ready and I was watching the second hand of my watch. Conditions could not have seemed less auspicious. It was the hottest July day of the century, the BBC said that evening. The sun stood molten above and scorched those fish. It was windless, breathless. I had greased a trout line, and mounted the wee doubles (size 14 and 16) which they used at Bridge of Dun. I could at least hope for a finnock.

I had six hours of almost continuous sport. Never before had I been a public entertainer except unintentionally when giving some solemn lecture. I do not know how much of the then narrow road got jammed with stopped cars. I suppose the spectators had baled out in the hope of seeing some gory motoring accident ahead. Anyway, that grassy verge was soon thick with holiday-makers. I did not mind their *watching*, after warning them to watch out for my back cast. What became a strain on the courtesy was the cross-examination; having to divide my attention between leaping seatrout and answering the interminable questions. With some, one didn't mind, like: 'What fly are they taking?' But: 'Where can I get a permit?' grew more and more tedious. The answer got abbreviated to: 'Sorry, you can't'.

I had known that those wee doubles sometimes took seatrout much bigger than finnock. It had not occurred to me that they might interest salmon. Five of my hours were up when I hooked one. With such fine tackle, I had to take *its* time. There was some cheering when it came ashore. Cameras clicked. I too felt cheered. I turned and smiled, for long enough to get an impression that a pipe-band was arriving. Some of the audience stood out (no room to stand apart) from the rest. Despite the torrid heat, they wore full highland dress, thick tweed jackets, bonnets, dirks, the lot; well, everything except plaids. When I was fishing again, I saw two huge kilties walk up the private path on the opposite bank studying not me but the water. At 6 p.m. precisely, having fought their way back through the crowd, they introduced themselves as the Balmoral ghillies; and took charge.

Now the right side from which to fish this pool – the 'Broad Pool' which is the best – is, unfortunately, the road side. It may have been the crowd which led the kilties to walk round to the wrong side, and to start fishing almost standing on the salmons' backs. This cannot, however, explain why they used large spinning rods armed with large prawns. I later learned that they had no luck. They did not really deserve to. I am sure they *meant* no harm, but the river was very low and they probably sent thousands of salmonidae back to the ocean, some stunned after banging their heads on the dam wall.

I met Mrs. Stirling at about 6.20 p.m. She was charming, and seemed pleased to receive the catch. Distant friends had been kept waiting for expected fish. She was very apologetic: her Morar hours for the rest of July were all bespoken – 'to those damned (name of city) Bailies who can't fish', she said; adding: 'Just wait until next summer'. I left feeling puzzled. Obviously the kilted gentlemen were not from *the* Balmoral, yet I felt sure that there was not another beat in Scotland of that name. Eventually the light dawned. Mrs. Stirling had been deceived: they were not ghillies either. They were too plump to see their sporrans without bending. They must have been Bailies *heavily* disguised.

Next summer was very different. I was not merely invited, I was in one sense incited. On the first morning, Mrs. Stirling's handsome daughter visited me early, on the bank. 'In this high water', she said, 'a worm will catch more salmon than a fly, and seatrout too'. I took the hint. Indeed, I had really no choice as she had brought some worms, and tarried a little to make sure that I did know how to use them. (I was reminded of Izaac Walton's encounters with 'the handsome Maudlin', though, unlike Maudlin, Miss Stirling did not burst into song.) Moreover, I was no longer rationed to six-hour stints, nor to one rod. When Jim came up for a week we were both welcomed. I think that we did what was hoped of us, though alas there was only one salmon that week. We learned the main snag about fishing below a Hydro-Electric dam – at unpredictable intervals they kept producing roaring albeit limpid floods, and each damned flood stopped all fish from taking fly for at least four hours.

The next two summers were much more productive. Less rain, and the Hydro-Electric had less surplus to discharge into the sea. It was now clear that my first Morar salmon on the wee double had been an Act of God. We found that the best way to get salmon for Mrs. Stirling's friends, was, despite the low water, her daughter's recipe. And this provided excitement too, as one's quarry was usually clearly visible. One could observe its increasing aggravation at the worm which kept swimming past its nose. But the best of it was the night fishing, once passing cars had stopped dazzling us and the fish, and other humans were in bed. For the first and only time, I caught a salmon (a grilse) in *total* darkness – in the middle of a moonless over-clouded night, when even the seatrout had become dormant. I have not read of this happening to anyone else, though it is not all that rare for seatrout fishers to catch salmon with some moonlight, or even just starlight. (This one *was* hooked in the mouth.)

My most vivid memory of the Morar is of the first time that the so-called 'dawn rise' really happened to me. I had so often tried to make it happen without success. Like that night at Grantown which we spent playing cards and drinking ale to stay awake; and then, in the dim light, night-vision not yet functioning properly, I fell slap on my face into the cold water as I stepped off the grass. *Too* much ale. Jim did not fall in, but he did not get an offer.

Judging by this first success, and a few which followed, for sea-trout at least 'dawn rise' is a misnomer. It should be 'pre-dawn' or 'first light'. Well before dawn it is over. The sky was so clear that night that it was never too dark to change a fly without a torch. I was fishing the lower ('Island') pool – rather mechanically, it was an hour and a half since I had felt a fish. When the water exploded near the far bank and my reel sang, I had not noticed the slight increase in visibility. It was a four-pounder. I must have been standing opposite a flotilla of four-pounders. Each time my No. 6 Butcher came within range of their vision, it was seized by the one quickest off the mark. It went on, according to my Record Book from 3.20 to 4 a.m. The last was a five pounder for a change, and since its predecessor had gone through a new hole in my net, it had to be lifted out by the gills. Activity stopped then, as abruptly as it started. I noticed at the time that my retinas were just beginning to detect colours.

I fished for another hour, but all was peace. I left with the first rays of the sun. That was a red-letter day-cum-night. Fishing alone, I got four salmon in the morning, rested for six hours while another guest fished; then, between 6 p.m. and 5 a.m., thirteen seatrout weighing 33 lb and twenty-five finnock. I expect I took it easy on the beach after that memorable session.

The fishery of another benefactor was *fairly* near to Morar as the eagle flies, though not to his home in the Borders. I had read his book, *Fishing From Afar*. It was written in a prison camp, and brims with nostalgia for the seatrout of Loch Coruisk in Skye. This reader at least got the impression that this inaccessible loch teemed with large seatrout. I had found that it would be possible to take a trippers' boat from Mallaig, camp by Coruisk, and return three days later. I wrote to Stephen Johnson to beg his leave to sample his loch. I cannot find his answer so I cannot check that I quote his exact words. After saying yes, he added that when writing his book, he had anticipated many letters which would say: 'Enjoyed your book. Please come and fish my water'; instead of which the many letters had (like mine) read: 'Enjoyed your book. Please may I fish *your* water'.

It was a mini-honeymoon. The weans were left in the care of a most reliable au pair girl. Our tent was pitched on the *machair* by the mouth of Coruisk burn. For three days of sun and zephyr, the only humans we saw were out on the decks of a couple of yachts, anchored for a night. The Cuillins are more dramatic when they are close above you. If I had thought that the loch might be empty we would have brought our climbing boots. Instead we lazed. Though late in July I never saw a fin in the loch, nor, more surprisingly, did high tides reveal any seatrout near the mouth of the burn. Our only deprivation was protein. We had the billy-cans, oatmeal, etc. but no fish to fry – except one mackerel.

It was a revelation when, spinning at the burn mouth with a little blue and silver, I hooked a tunny – or so it seemed from the length and power of its initial run. It was a one-pound mackerel. Weight for weight it far outclassed any fish that I have played. There is a lesson here. What a waste of sport it had been when, as a boy, I went out in boats at dusk with fishermen of Oronsay and of Arran. We simply hoisted the mackerel into the boat, usually two at a time, on stout canes and with a bit of seagull's feather on each hook. Food fishing. When seatrout are extinct, which will not take long if the runs continue to dwindle, there is this alternative. Catch your mackerel on a light trout fly rod, and a demon type lure with long white feathers. You will get a surprise. And freshly cooked mackerel is just as tasty as seatrout. Indeed more so to my salmon-jaded palate.

On the Taymount stretch of the Tay

1955 was the end for the summer free fishers on the Tay. The Tay Salmon Fisheries Company must also have noticed the increasing runs of summer fish. It had the angling rights on the left bank from Cargill down and decided to let them. Gloom for the Mundle brothers, and many others: except the two other brothers who won the competition to become tenants, respectively, of Cargill and Stobhall. Jim and I also competed. I could not, however, have made much use of the prize, had we won. For the lets stretched all the way from mid-January to mid-August. It was a much heavier blow for Jim who was not in exile.

He chanced to hear, however, that Taymount House and fishing had been let to a Mr. George D. Macbeth from mid-May until mid-August. Jim donned his kilt and knocked at the front door of Taymount House. He had flown with Canadian squadrons and had adventured for over a year in and around Vancouver. Mr. Macbeth's fortune had been made in Canada. They hit it off. Jim came away with the freedom to use Taymount/Stobhall, after Mr. Macbeth had finished his days on this water. He was no fanatic. He finished his fishing days at exactly 3.30 p.m. Jim was a fast worker and usually, thereafter, managed to get his summer day's work done by soon after 3 p.m. Mr. Macbeth was as generous to me, when I met him at the beginning of August. Yes, of course, I could join Jim during the next two weeks. We had again fallen on our feet. And we stayed on them until Jim's tragic death in 1962; which was soon followed by that of our most munificent benefactor. Even when we caught more than he did, Mr. Macbeth would never accept a fish. The disparity was sometimes considerable. It would sometimes have been embarrassing if, as I think he should have done, he had asked us to report our catches. He was above such trivia. It did not even occur to him, or to us, that his signature on a piece of paper might some day be needed.

This omission was to cause me inconvenience, once. I was fishing the Aldern Stream alone. As I banged the head of the second salmon, a line of men came over the top, through the alder trees on the high bank behind me, and lunged down at me. When I had recovered from my fright, one had a firm grip on the fish, and one on my rod. A third was the spokesman. He had every right to be – he was Mr. MacRae's successor. His profession as water bailiff had made him less than trusting. His ace of trumps was: 'So you say. Let us call on Mr. Macbeth'. I think that my ready compliance, and my wish to leave my rod among the trees, dented his confidence. He got more polite. I kicked myself later for forgetting to ask him to carry my first fish to my car. They overlooked it lying quite close on the bank. Fortunately Mr. Macbeth was at home. Apologies were profuse. They were called for, too. I had wasted an hour. Fortunately the fish were still in a self-sacrificial mood when I got back to the Alderns.

For the next seven years, my fishing holidays on the Tay were relatively restful – I could rest during the mornings. The six hours till about 9.30 p.m. provided enough exercise to keep one's muscles in training. Even with the help of my detailed Record Books, it is difficult to select from my many happy memories. Here goes. It was an advantage to have seen the skeleton of the Tay in 1955, the summer when it almost dried up completely. One could then, dry shod, inspect the places where fish lay when the gauge was at zero. It was a big surprise to find that in the middle of the river bed over 100 yards wide, there was a deep channel of about fifteen yards wide, often girt by sharp rock. (By September in 1955, the water level was sinking even in that channel.) This explained Grimble's account of how, harling at Cargill, he lost five three-inch flies ('Eagles') in rapid succession, his cast cut on rock by October fish. For those who wade deep, the more you know about the river bed the better, and the safer.

In those days, the British summer had not become one prolonged drought. One could rely on some floods in July to stock the river. If fly fishers were lucky, the 'Lammas floods' did not come, as Grimble says, *during* the first half of August. I did not mind how much rain came after that. A very great virtue of the Stobhall/Taymount water is that it provides good fly fishing at a fairly wide range of water levels. I shall not divulge all of my hard-earned knowledge, but I will offer some gifts. When it is six to twelve inches too high for fly on the Aldern Stream, Stankend is at its best. When it drops too low for Stankend, the Alderns is at its best. (About Willie's Stane and the Cubby-Hole, find out for yourself, if you get the chance). On the lower beat, apart from 1955, it cannot get too low for 'No Man's Land' – the top half-mile, never penetrated by boats.

No. I must qualify that 'never'. In August 1976, as I fished at Stankend, a blue speck far down-stream gradually got larger. An hour later, it turned out to be a light single seater rowing boat being pulled up those rapids, single-handed, by a well-built gentleman. When he reached the foot of Stankend, he waded, without waders, half-way across the rapids, anchored the boat, let out about forty yards of rope and fished alternatively with two rods, *standing up*. I watched with bated breath. His fly, then spinner, then fly were covering the top of the Top Pocket. A fish hooked there if, as usual, large, invariably runs down-stream. Was he planning to swim down after it? I did not find out. He did retrieve his anchor, which I had not expected. I think he earned the Order of the Bath.

No Man's Land is adventurous water – very fast, with deep pockets and big boulders. I have fished it for over twenty-five years; yet during every low water visit, I have learned some new lie, or some fly water that had previously seemed impossible to reach. And when the water is warm (it reached 70° in my week in 1975!) this is where the takers are to be found. I have given names to the casts and lies in No Man's Land, a dignity not conferred by the fishing maps, and they deserve it: 'Top Pocket', 'Four-Grilse Point', 'Sangster's Run', 'Fail-me-Never'. They might catch on. Perhaps Harry is passing them on. Fishing friends need names for ease of reference. I shall tell you a little about Four-Grilse Point, where you are least likely to drown.

I christened it after catching there four grilse in about ten casts. (It has not happened again. Yet.) It is debatable whether I should have called those fish 'grilse'. They were like average grilse in length, but each weighed between ten and eleven pounds. I have never seen such fat salmon. At Four-Grilse Point there is barely twenty yards of fishing water, which starts higher up than you would expect. Fish lie and show below that gravel spit with the sandy bay below it, but very rarely do they take there, except at dusk. It should be fished inch by inch until you are casting as long a line as you can throw. The best of the water is churned up by boulders and in low water a No. 8 on the tail is recommended, and a 10 on the dropper for the not so few fish which prefer it to a No. 8. It is, admittedly, a place where the second fly is liable to get snagged. But the losses so caused are appreciably fewer than the gains due to the dropper.

On this issue I think I have converted all my fishing friends except Harry. Unfortunately for him, though not the fish, he introduced his dropper fly in the shallow water of Dess. I fear that he blames me for the series of fish which he proceeded to lose, with the free fly snagged on boulders. He'll come round to it on the Tay. It is different there, in pools where the strength of the current will keep your tail fly riding high. There are, of course, various pools where using a dropper would be madness, like Upper Eels Brigs waded from the right bank. There fish try to run forthwith down out of the tail, even when hooked 100 yards above it. It may take about five minutes of careful wading until you get back down to the part where you can wade ashore; and then, if your fish stays on for long enough to grow weary, you still have to negotiate it over that bouldery, weedy, up and down shelf. I reckon that I have done reasonably well if I land half the fish hooked there. Unless of course the water is about two feet high on gauge, when you need only wade a few yards, and fish run and rest within easy range.

In those earlier days I still used 'grease' (Mucilin) on a Kingfisher line. It was messy. The stuff was transferred from fingers to cast, and I would then try to get it off with docken leaves. (I never got round to Fuller's Earth, whatever that is.) But the system worked, especially in Stankend, from the left bank, in the middle and lower parts where the surface is smooth; and there the fish behaved *à la* Wood. It was the nearest that I ever got, when salmon fishing, to the continuous excitement of trout fishing during a real 'rise'. The salmon, of course, are much less predictable, but I remember evenings, weeks, when I could rely on the first time down Stankend giving half a dozen mere swirls *plus* another half-dozen 'contacts', the latter to be duly divided, rather irregularly, between 'Pulls', 'Hook Came Out' and 'Landed'. It seems a long time since it went like that. I fear that I may have to revert to that messy grease.

It was odd that when Jim and I fished together, we scarcely ever did equally well. Either it was his day or it was my day, with scores like 3–0, or 5–1: though it evened out when we later worked out the totals. There were, of course days when we tied 0–0. It was also odd that he got so many in the 30 to 36-lb range, and my best was, and remains, 26 lb. I sometimes felt indignant. Now I am resigned, having had twenty-six pounders in half a dozen rivers. We were born under different stars. Without being unco-operative, we were a bit competitive. (It was worse when shooting, when he liked to show me that he was quicker on the draw. He was, and I did not want so much proof.) Fortunately, when the water level suited each pool, as it often did, he preferred Stankend and I the Alderns. So we did not get in each other's way, and we exchanged blow-by-blow accounts on the road back to Dundee. Sometimes I still go down to Stankend, though doing well enough in the Alderns, to catch fish that he should still be catching. *In memoriam*. He'd prefer it to flowers.

In later years, when I had to pay for the Tay, and was a bankman for George Mann, I sometimes made George cross. By nature, I am not an early riser. He was. If I arrived at the Taymount hut after 9 a.m., he would be spinning from the boat in the Findford Stream; and I knew it would be about 10.30 when I got rowed across. Fair enough. My punishment for being a layabed. I sat and smoked, and watched the boat. On these occasions it was *always* sunny. Subconsciously (is the 'sub' honest?) I hoped that their view of me might make it a ten o'clock ferry. George would shout 'Fish' (the imperative verb) . . . 'lots of water' . . . 'above me'. I never heard all of it on account of the roar of that turbulent stream. I would shake my head. No wonder he was irritated. It *looks* marvellous water. But in the many years that I have fished there, the boat never got a fish in the first hour and a half. If they could not succeed, with the still low sun behind their backs, what chance had I, since my fly would approach a fish's sun-blinded eye! Despite delay, including a mile's walk upstream, I wanted to be in No Man's Land while the sun angle was ideal for the left side. Even after my late arrivals, which left less than two hours' fishing time before I was back for the lunch-time ferry, I averaged two to three morning fish. The time for fly from the croys on the right bank of Findford Stream is when the sun has gone off the water. But for the opportunities to explore and experiment which I owe to Mr. Macbeth, what a lot of time and energy I would have wasted later, when my fishing was no longer a gift from the gods, via him.

On the Tay at Ballathie

Those who fish the Tay only in early spring or autumn, in the stretches suited for harling, could never guess how many good trout lie hidden in this river. They live in the shallower broken water, which used to boil with feeding fish when the flies were hatching in later April and in May. Yet few trout fishers would then turn out, at least on the Ballathie water. This was then owned by the late Colonel J. S. L. Hardie. Having retired from his post as Chairman of the Steel

Board his main ambition was to capture a monster salmon; like those fifty-pounders whose plaster casts adorn a room in his former home – the room which is now the bar of Ballathie House Hotel.

He went on trying occasionally during the early summer when the free fishers were out in force. He wielded a big fly rod, normally from the boat. He deserved a boatman better versed in the ways of salmon – he was often casting his flies in unpromising places. His boatman kept in the boat at least two anchors. I suppose that the Colonel bought them by the dozen, for his boatman had a flair for finding boulders which trapped anchors. Once in May, I saw him fail to retrieve two within half an hour. When the rope had been cut for the second time, the boat was beached and I had my first chat with the Colonel.

Having made his acquaintance, I felt that politeness required that I formally seek his permission to fish for Ballathie trout. I knew that he would not, even if he could, debar trout fishers from his water. However, during May one might still meet a bailiff or his 'watcher' who sometimes sought to chase away even an angler casting flies for trout. Permission was readily granted. I had no more need to argue with a watcher about my right to try for a trout before the spring salmon lettings ended on Cargill.

The Cargill/Ballathie water contains two fine stretches for the trout. One is the strong streamy water below Cargill Viaduct. Better still is the top 100 yards of the lower beat from the left bank. I christened this 'Egg Run'. It bordered on Willie's hen farm, and Willie kindly let me take my car to his cottage, a stone's throw from the river. In May those trout used to drive me mad. I waded knee-deep and all around the trout were sipping down floating flies. I kept on and on changing patterns, all ignored by the bigger fish and rarely sampled even by the smaller. Sometimes, having waded down all of the trout-congested stretch, I would reach, in quieter water, a shoal of grayling. They were too easy to catch, when in the mood. One then had a touch from nearly every cast and about a third were hooked. This was no consolation. I then despised the grayling, which had not yet recovered from spawning.

At last, in 1954, I made a breakthrough. I abandoned the wet flies which had served me so well in many rivers and lochs, and had proved much more productive than my dilatory dabbles with a dry fly. I acquired some Martin's Parachute flies and they earned their keep. I found that even I could make them stay afloat with wings held high; and one pattern was enough – Greenwell's Glory, for it was usually Olive Duns which triggered those explosive rises. In the arts of dry fly fishing I did not attain the skill of a keen Winchester schoolboy. Still, I did at last land a few of the big trout, big at least by my standards – up to two pounds. I did not catch as many as my friend A, whose summer speciality was swimming a wasp grub. I never acquired the courage to try to rob the wasps.

I owe more to Colonel Hardie. But for him, I should later have pined away two summers without even one week of salmon fishing on the Tay. Mr. Macbeth had died and I had not yet met George Mann. It seemed hopeless – until I heard from a friend that the Colonel's health was failing a bit and he might be willing to let his water for the odd week. He kindly let me have, for a modest rent, a week in each September. This is not, in my experience, a reliable fishing month on the Tay. The lower beats, including Ballathie, are then chock full of salmon. Except in floods, they are forever leaping and lunging. Yet their interest in lures is unpredictable – sometimes suicidal, sometimes dour.

In that first September week our bag was respectable, but alas it was spinning water, yet not quite high enough for Egg Run – a prolific stretch with a big spoon in a raging flood, when the running salmon rest in what in May are trout-filled shallows. Next year, the water level was ideal for the fly. The week started splendidly for me, with six good salmon in the morning from the viaduct run. I fished there throughout two more mornings with the Colonel standing above me on the viaduct to watch the sport – and I did not get an offer. I prefer the climax to come at the end of a week of fishing.

My friend A owes more to the Colonel than I do. He lives not far from Ballathie, and when the Colonel's boatman was not busy on the river he used to visit A occasionally, for a listener and preferably also a drink. He once spent the whole of an afternoon sheltering there from a cloud-burst, and then invited A to come and have a cast. At his third or fourth cast A hooked a portmanteau fish, which was duly landed. Its plaster cast, even bigger than those in Ballathie House, now decorates his drawing room. A and his monster were, of course, photographed. Somehow one of these pictures found its way into the pages of *Trout and Salmon*. Somehow, but not from his boatman, it reached the Colonel's ears just where this fish had been caught. The boatman, now in a panic, told A that his job was in jeopardy as that invitation had been 'unofficial'. A was invited to Ballathie House. He accepted with some trepidation. He need not have worried. The Colonel found A a man of his own heart. They did have a heart to heart talk – about fish and fishing, lubricated with whisky. A's later invitations to fish Ballathie were official. And the boatman was forgiven. I take off my hat to the Colonel, a generous sportsman. He had spent many years trying for a Tay leviathan, yet *his* biggest fish weighed less than thirty pounds.

Around a hill loch near Stranraer

My boldness in seeking permission to fish might not have developed, but for my first, modest success. That benefactor's name is long forgotten, but I remember writing 'J.P.' after it when I wrote to him at the age of thirteen. It was during my first fishing holiday, when I did nothing else. I had been packed off for some fresh air. That first winter of yellow Glasgow fogs, after breathing clean east coast air, had not suited my health. I am afraid that they must have been sea-trout parr on which I practised first with my fly rod in a sluggish burn. Then I had cycled up over moorlands, without a rod, to look at a small loch shown on the map. It was early April. I saw nothing rising, but I heard a very English voice call ' . . . beautiful head and tail rise'. In a bay round a bend, I watched, from a respectful distance, two men casting. I think it was from the Post Office that I discovered the owner of that loch. My letter got a prompt and affirmative reply – for one named day.

When, later, I had got spoiled, I would not if you paid me repeat that day. But then – it made my holiday. Despite the cold wind, the sullen sky, and the total absence of rising trout, I was happy proceeding round the edge, expecting with every cast a 'head and tail rise', but uncertain what it would look like. After the midday break, I scanned my small collection of flies. It contained one excellent imitation of a large black beetle, bought from Martin's and not yet tried. Perhaps the trout were eating such objects down below. I let it sink a bit in the peaty water. It happened. My first pounder. It felt like a whale compared with those parr. That kept me going until it was nearly dark when I caught its twin. I nearly burst with pride, free wheeling down the hill towards the twinkling lights of Stranraer. They ate well too.

Next Easter Jim came with me and we discovered what turned out to be the Stranraer Reservoir. There were no 'No Fishing' notices. He caught his first trout on a fly called 'the Professor'. Fortunately it was near the end of the week before an official discovered us; and told us, not unkindly, that he thought *everyone* knew that fishing there was not allowed.

But it does not always work

Even with my luck, sometimes 'Yes' meant 'No'. The example which

I choose to illustrate this will serve another purpose – to show that I am not a salmonidae snob. Far from it. Otherwise I would not have had one top of my first fly rod broken by youngsters to whom I taught the simplest way of catching pike.

I shall indicate the breadth of my angling interests by reference to *big* game fishing – sharks *à la* Hemingway. I owe it to my long-suffering wife to give her a *real* holiday now and then. For, her, it does not count as such unless we get at least half-way to the equator, to where the sun is so hot that she has to seek shade, and sun-bathes by proxy. (I am proxy.) Naturally I have tried to arrange these trips in late March or September. Sometimes they have had to be when the seatrout and grilse were running. Then, I have found as I frizzle that no literature, light or heavy, can keep my thoughts off those fish. This time we hired a Mini in Lisbon – in July! Sheila does meet me half-way – visits to *inland* castles, volcanoes, deserts, etc., must be few and brief. When frizzled, I need sea cooling.

The hotel in Lisbon had a brochure proclaiming Portugal as *the* country for shark fishers. I made a mental note that two of the top centres for this sport happened to lie on our route towards the equator. Before registering at the glossy hotel at the first such centre, I luckily learnt that no sharks had been landed there for months. We meandered south to the second centre. Assuming that the large hotel would organise such sport, we booked in; only to find that the shark fishing was organised (if that is not too generous a verb) by a polyglot, who also organised drinking, and much besides. Despite the fact that he had started on Schnapps just after breakfast, he was able to promise to organise your shark at any hour and, it seemed, in any language. But when tomorrow came, 'tomorrow' always turned out to be the *next* day.

Well, it could not have been a nicer place to wait, buoyed by expectancy. Each day we found a new bay below cliffs with sands untouched by human foot, caves wherein Sheila could shelter from the sun, and Atlantic breakers to dive through. During the second half of the week we were reduced to a bed and breakfast place with just enough room to squeeze round the bed. But Sheila too had read Hemingway and understood that some sacrifices have to be made. To keep me on the boil the Schnapps man had thrown in *free* what he described as 'an afternoon's fishing' for – well, whatever might take hold of a bait trolled at twenty knots in a 'pleasure' boat full of people whose language I never identified. One fish was hooked, but the excitable guide beat me to it (the rod). With his triumphant exuberance, no northern Celt could compete. If it was a shark, it was not yet weaned.

After a week we were getting restless. We still had other sights to see. At last Old Schnapps made a firm commitment. It seemed a bit of a come-down. Not a shark expedition after all. He had for days been trying to divert me to the bass. I had dismissed them, catchable in the Menai Straits. I had, however, been slow to realise that ten kilos – the average weight, he said, of the promised dozen – is over twenty pounds. I agreed to meet the Germans at 2.30 a.m. (so early because of the tide.) They turned up at 3.30 a.m. It was only when our motor boat was chugging out of the harbour, and I was watching the twinkling lights of returning fishing boats, that the German who had a little English asked me 'vair ist your rod?' *Donner und Blitzen*! Old Schnapps had promised to *hire* me all the tackle, as the brochure said he would. He had forgotten of course, and it was too late and too early to persuade his staff to dare to return and let me try to waken him.

Actually it turned out better to be rodless. The kindest German let me hold his for a little while, after it was clear that we were in the wrong place. The right places were within 100 yards of the foot of the 100 yard high cliff. One bolder crew of professional fishers were catching a few fifty yards nearer to the cliff. Our crew were not taking the risk. (I'll explain this shortly.)

I had said to myself 'to hell with fishing', and had given myself up to a Wordsworthian communion with nature. The stars were fading, the black cliffs towered above, and soon even the Germans were speechless (with disappointment). Stillness among the gulls and lapping waves. At first I thought it was due to some retinal malfunction – I *seemed* to see, dimly, white shapes ascending the vertical cliff. A little later I was sure that I saw one falling back and landing with a splash. As the light grew stronger I definitely discerned tiny objects moving up there on the skyline. It was still some time before I identified these shapes as human and could see their very long rods.

I then had an hour of vicarious excitement. They hurled out a large herring plus a pound or two of lead, and much later, parabola completed, it hit the Atlantic. That was why *our* crew kept their distance. Now just imagine winding a twenty pounder or even a ten pounder up 100 yards of vertical cliff! To reduce losses those sportsmen had an ingenious device, which I cannot describe in detail, as I never got close enough to it. They fished in pairs. When a bass had been hooked and played, a large wicker-work basket was somehow attached so that it slid down the line, and, with luck, entrapped more than half of the thrashing fish, and absorbed the bangs against the rocky ledges. About half of the bass dropped off during their upward journey, including most of those where the basket had failed to slide over the fish. But some anglers lost fish plus basket. The Bass King became visible later. He had descended, presumably by rope, to a little ledge on the water's edge. His sport was incessant. He pulled them in over seaweeded rocks. Each time he did an arm dance for the benefit of the mugs in the boats. He once fell in. He got out so soon that he *must* have been roped.

I meant to reach the cliff top next dawn before we left, to study this novel technique. I slept too late. I did however look down the little fish scaled gully where they slid the fish up the last lap. The cliffs really were as vertical as they had looked from below. I would love to try it, but I would want a rod of at least twenty feet, and a boy with a cool head to report on the progress of an ascending fish. Though I never saw a shark, I did at least get some good colour slides of sword-fish, being unloaded from boats at the water's edge. One had to waste a lot of film to get a few pictures which showed only fish plus boats or fishermen, and not the other tourists who, like me, were milling around with cameras.

3
Some True Fishing Stories

We all know the innuendo in 'fishing story'. I can vouch for the truth of the following. I do not need to fib or even exaggerate, though in one case, I suspect, I may have added a stitch or two of embroidery.

The Policeman's beat
John had leased Taymount House and fishing for a few weeks, and had advertised for paying guests. I seized the chance of a week in late July. It was marvellous living in that mansion, furnished in exquisite taste, overlooking Campsie Lynn. Two bonnie, genteel lassies slaved for us, fetching hot lunches to the fishing huts and cooking us five-star dinners. John made a loss that week, for the only guests were myself and an elderly angler who, fortunately for me, preferred boat fishing. In effect, I had the water to myself. Dinners were unhurried and the conversation so enjoyable that, though the fishing was very productive, I never went back for an evening cast. Assuming that none of John's later guests would do so either, I 'phoned him during his last week in August and offered to fish for him some evening. (John had kept the right to use one rod.) I was invited for Saturday.

I was sure that the Alderns had been flogged all day, for the boats are kept there and the new boatman conserved his energies for whatever he did in his evenings. I decided to rest it for a while and started at the bottom of the beat. Stankend yielded two fish to 'Dessy'. (Dessy is now deceased. It was the fly pattern on which Harry got his first Dee fish, and he gave me a couple of the dozen which he had then had tied.) I lost a whopper below the Kilmou hut: when ready for beaching, it found the barbed wire which some clot had chucked in the river when rewiring the fence. As I waded out to the top of the Alderns at 7 p.m., I was startled to see a boat being rowed across the water which I had been resting, then heading up my side to where I stood, about to start. 'We're going to fish here', said the burliest of the pair in the boat. 'Sorry', I said, 'I've been asked to fish by and for the tenant'. The answer was 'So have we.' I could not disprove it, though I did not really believe it; nor that he was, as he said, 'Jock Smith'. At last I won a battle of will and they went up to fish below Willie's Stane.

It was one of those rare evenings when you never get out a full fly line before you are into another salmon. At 8 p.m. I had only waded the top ten yards and was down again by the beaching bay, fighting it out with the third large fish (not counting the earlier brace). Glancing up-stream I was startled again to see the second Taymount boat crossing, well loaded, towards Willie's Stane. Shortly later, I had, for ten minutes, to divide my attention between an obstinate salmon and *John's paying guests*. Unexpectedly, having spun all week for nothing and desperate for a fish to take home, they had spurned the five-course dinner, grabbed a quick bite and returned. John had not seen them to tell them that he had invited me. You can imagine their manic fury, having passed four big fish on the bank (two near Willie's Stane) before reaching me. A polite answer usually turns away wrath – but it was very slow to work this time. The burly man had followed them down, and kept echoing the things I said – 'fishing for John', 'you take him these fish', etc.

When my fish was at last despatched, and my identity documented, an uneasy peace returned. I offered to lend them my fly rod, but they could not use it. I left them to fish the middle part of the Alderns where, I advised them, a spinner had the best chance, and then went up to the tail of the glide above, the Cubby Hole. Into a grilse at once. And then I saw the burly boy wading in only twenty yards below one of the guests. That proved that he was no friend of John's. I deliberately broke with the grilse. With all haste, and keeping out of sight, I collected the brace I had caught in Stankend, fortunately left above the alder trees. I panted up the brae to my car and hurtled to Taymount House. In by the back door, I dumped the brace in the kitchen and yelled for John. Within the minute he was off to investigate.

As he told me later, that lazy boatman had been inviting *his* evening guests. Whether he rented the boat key could not be proved. It was the end for him. The boldness of the burly 'Smith' was explained – he was a police constable. He clearly knew that water well. I wonder which fishing beat became his next evening beat.

Introducing Harry to the Tay

I had tried to achieve this for twenty-five years before I succeeded. I had then resigned myself to Harry remaining a one river man, now

Taymount water. Above: Campsie Lynn viewed from Taymount House.
Below: The Taymount side of Findford Stream.

At the top of Cargill Viaduct Stream.

The cast from below Willie's Stane. *Steve Wallace*

Fishing the Aldern Stream: two views. *Steve Wallace*

wed to the Dee. Then in 1973, he 'phoned at rather short notice. The grouse apparently were scarce. I was about to fish Stobhall, in the second week of August as one of George Mann's bank rods, and I sought permission for Harry to fish my rod on Tuesday. Of course George said that both of us must fish. It was the upper beat that day. Now Harry had been an over-generous host on the Dee, always insisting ('guests do what they're told') that I fish well-stocked Kincardine while he searched the pools of upper Dess. At last it was my turn to tell him where to fish. I'd had six fish on Monday and wanted to arrange a day which would not disappoint him. With so much lovely fly water, it was, of course, no sacrifice to have him be the first to fish in each of my favourite streams. I had not, however, intended to end up *quite* so far in arrears, with one fish to his seven. Still, they were all grilse. He had not yet felt the power of a big one in these strong currents. When we shared the grilse with George, I asked tentatively if he would mind if Harry rejoined us on Saturday.

That was his *real* introduction, though for him it started tamely. As six of Harry's seven grilse had come from Stankend, I thought that it was in his interests to have it to himself that morning, but the river was a crucial few inches lower. He returned, clean, at 12.30, in time to witness my fourth battle with a twenty-pounder, from each of whose jaws the No. 10 Drury fly tore out after about fifteen minutes. A school of newly arrived fish had started showing at about 10 a.m. all over the lower Alderns. George, from the boat, had tried unsuccessfully to tempt them with all sorts of large spinners. The wee Drury flies did not get a deep enough hold.

But I too was to blame. Two of my four bereavements, including the one which Harry witnessed, involved fish running out of the pool; and as they passed the bottom croy my line caught round an unfamiliar underwater boulder. Each time I managed to release the line, after some dicy wading and much rod waving, but only after a minute or so of excessive strain. In all of my years there this had never happened before, and I followed my habit of wading ashore and following the fish by walking down the vestigial path. I should have learnt my lesson the first time, at most the second. Believe it or not, mindless habit led me to lose another big fish in the same way that evening. Observant Harry had got the solution in one. When his chances came later with big fish running out of the pool, he stayed in the river, wading as deep as possible, and *his* line never touched that boulder, now happily departed.

Harry is well endowed with what Aristotle called 'practical reason'. But his sport did not start until tea-time. We all fished the

Alderns and Willie's Stane, but the fish seemed asleep that hot afternoon. They started to show again near the tail of the Alderns while the boat was having its last cast in the middle of that pool. I tied on a No. 1 Hairy Mary double, and tried it at the tail. Success at last – I beached two fifteen-pounders in about fifteen minutes. Then I rushed up to give Harry another such fly. Almost at once a fish took fifty yards off his reel. The fly came back with only one hook. I have not known it happen before or since. As later dissection revealed, the hook soldered on to make it a double had just come off. (Rust?) Harry teased me: 'So that's the sort of fly you keep for guests'. I gave him the one from my own rod (having plenty more).

When George and the boatmen departed at 5 p.m. it was my custom to repair to Perth for an early grill and get back for the last two hours of light. But Harry's blood was up. He persuaded me that there were enough scraps in our picnic baskets to keep us going a little longer. I gave in, since the wallopers were now showing all over the Alderns. We both used big flies, though Harry found later that a No. 6 Drury sufficed. When the sky was almost black, Harry made it a tie – six fish apiece. But he was Top Dog again on weight; and my six were from eleven prolonged encounters, his from only seven (excluding, as we must, the one with 'the guest fly'). I was lying on the bank exhausted during his final battle. Though we had given some to George, each of us had to carry nearly seventy pounds of salmon up the stiff climb to the cars, easier when you can see the rabbit holes. Harry's sack had collapsed on trying to lift it. Host or not, I had to leave him to go back and collect them in a spare sack fetched from the car. Six consecutive days of fly fishing, day and evening, takes its toll. As we parted I said: 'I don't suppose you'll want to come back'. Reply: 'Just try to stop me'.

There has been no stopping him. The following autumn *he* fell on his feet – he was invited to be bank rod for a party which takes for a fortnight both Cargill and Stobhall. In 1975 the second half of September got Noah's Ark weather. No one but a mad Englishman who had not yet fished the Tay in raging flood would have considered putting up a fly rod. He did and persisted – and thus caught twenty-two, averaging 16 lb, the best weighing 33, *all on the same individual fly:* a No. 2 Stoat's Tail, now very bedraggled. (He is so blasé that he has not framed it.) On days when the river was too high, even by his standards, i.e. over eight feet on the gauge, he introduced the Tay salmon to the fat Blair spoon, and thereby got fourteen. Surprisingly, these ran smaller than his fly-caught fish, averaging a mere 13½ lb. He is now another Tay addict.

It was a bit demoralising for me. I had waited twenty-five years for the chance to be able to teach Harry *something* – a thing or two about big river fishing; then found him teaching me. I refer not only to that boulder, resting temporarily on its way to the sea. It was Harry who demonstrated to me that No. 10 Drury flies will catch big Tay fish. But my most humbling lesson was on how to catch the fish which lie about four yards below Willie's Stane, almost in reach (I suppose; I have not tried) of a long-handled gaff. The problem for me, and the scores of other anglers I have seen tantalised there, is that the salmon lie too close to that gigantic boulder for one to present to them a fly, as distinct from a rod tip.

The answer, which should have been obvious to anyone with eyes, was spotted at once by Harry – a wadeable, if narrow, ledge runs up the outside of the Stane. So, leaning against those tons of granite, you can get out some line as well as the cast before the fly has passed the lie. Harry made the point by deeds not words. I was seated on the bank when he hooked his first, a fifteen-pounder, and he had beached two more like it within about half an hour. I was not alone in my shame. I had been joined by S, a former free fisher, who was waiting for us to go and enjoy our sumptuous dinner at Ballathie House. S and I then spent twenty minutes in the Alderns, not watching our own lines, but cricking our necks to watch Harry playing his fish. S knows this beat better than I do, but he too had never before seen a fish taken on fly where Harry hooked those three.

I *think*, however, that I may at last have taught Harry something. He is much too polite to tell me so if he knew it already. Perhaps he had decided that it was my turn for a fish. It was on Friday this summer. Self-effacingly, I had invited the other two fly men to have first-down-the-Alderns on Monday and Wednesday. Feeling that the Lord owed me a reward, I flogged it throughout Friday morning, fruitlessly: to learn from the boatmen at lunch that the river had been rising slowly and was up by six inches. Those Hydro-Electric spoil-sports could surely afford to send a helicopter down the river from the dam at Pitlochry, to warn anglers to have a four-hour rest. The effect of their discharge is not obvious to wading anglers about twenty miles down-stream, but it is as disastrous as those sudden torrents in the Morar.

Throughout lunch I kept a close watch on some shingle, up which the water was still slowly creeping. At 2.15 p.m. we were all still lolling, joking, digesting. Nonchalantly I picked up my fly rod, and said 'It will be falling soon. We'll catch something this afternoon.' This was disingenuous, for I had seen that it had *just started* to drop (by a quarter of an inch). I went in at the top of the Alderns, instead of inviting one of the others. The next half-hour was the only half-hour that week that any of us had it fast and furious. The big one was so furious that it attached my tail fly to a distant boulder, chewed out the dropper and left for me a lump of moss. After two less frustrating tussles, I did at least atone by bawling to David, fishing below me, to come above me before it was all over. He was a bit slow in responding – but just in time to catch one with his first cast. Harry had sensibly hastened down-river to Stankend where the extra six inches of water usually makes all the difference. But the small run of tide-ies had by then passed Stankend. I expect Harry did know that 'secret', but in case others do not: in these Hydro-Electric freshets or floods, rest so long as the water is rising, but waste not a second when it starts to drop.

Great-Gran's way with salmon

My mother-in-law is a remarkable woman. She suddenly became a salmon-fisher thirty years ago when a youngster of fifty-five. She still displays her spinning rod conspicuously at home – a hint, I think, that invitations are welcome. It started on the Orton beat on the Spey, then rented by her husband. Visiting him one baking August afternoon, she was disgusted to find the men-folk sunbathing with no fish on the bank. She picked up the nearest spinning rod and got the ghillie to show her how to use it. To everyone's astonishment she was, almost immediately, into a fish which was ultimately landed. She did much the same to me a few years later on the Spey, on Major Dunbar's water. We had fished without reward from 9 a.m. until noon, when I advised her that the sun was now shining so much down-stream that it was a waste of time to continue. But we needn't leave for lunch for half an hour, she replied. I left her to fish the lower part of a pool where I had never seen a fish. I lay in the lush grass. Next time I looked her way, her rod was bending. We were *very* late for lunch. She insisted on playing the fish her way, and it took about five minutes per pound before the twelve-pounder was ashore. I christened it 'Gran's Pool'.

I shall tell you about the most remarkable day's fishing that we shared, when again she wiped my eye; and also that of a Minister of the Kirk. It was on Upper Stobhall, on one of those days when the river was clear but too high for its fly casts, yet not quite high enough to force fish in near the bank. On such a day, harling comes into its own for those who have a taste for it. Jim and I never did, so Gran shared the boat with the Minister. They abandoned spinning from the boat fairly soon. She was unaccustomed to casting alternately with another rod, and Bob, the boatman, had patiently sorted out some tangles. At lunch we were all fishless, and only a few big running fish had been showing in mid-stream. I then replaced the huge spinner, which she had been lent by Bob, with a two-inch Brown and Gold wooden devon. (When I have to spin the Tay in summer, I find that unless the water is coloured, spinners of 1½–2 in. do better than the larger lures normally used.) The boat harled its way down to the Kilmou hut, and when I saw them coming ashore for a rest, I followed down-stream to cadge a lift to the opposite bank.

The Minister drew me aside. 'She's an obstinate old besom' he said, and added: 'I've got a lot like her in my parish'. It emerged that during the last hour, she had had three pulls, taking line off her tensionless reel; ignoring urgent advice to wrap her line round the stone provided for this purpose, and prop her rod on the wooden spiggot. 'I always hold the rod in my hand' was all the change they got. I surreptitiously tightened the tension on her revolving drum reel, and after being ferried, left them to it. For the rest of the story, I rely on testimony of the others, as I spent about an hour playing a big fish out of sight down-stream. (It earned its freedom by getting the line round a rock and breaking it.) When I returned at tea-time, I was astonished to learn that Gran had caught two fish, of 15 and 20 lb. And the Minister had still had no offers. It is the twenty-pounder which shows her uncanny flair for hooking fish.

She was a bit puzzled about this harling business. At the mid-afternoon rest she had asked me why the boat kept going round in circles. Shortly after resuming she said to Bob: 'Isn't my line pointing the wrong way?' It was indeed – her devon had caught a rock twenty yards or more up-stream. 'Gie it a good tug and it'll come free', said Bob. At the third tug, after a momentary pause, her reel started whizzing, and the boat was hastily pulled to the bank. Fortunately she had a lot of line on that reel, and Jim, on seeing her stumbling up the bank, made haste to join her. When the line was almost exhausted, she had the good sense to hand him the rod, saying: 'You can run faster than I can.' He just managed to save the situation, but it was nearly an hour later before the fish *hooked in the tail* was netted. It had been resting behind that rock! Jim was exhausted by that battle, as he had just finished playing two sixteen-pounders in close succession before starting the marathon. Still Gran won on weight, and I believe that her friends were duly impressed next day when she showed them her catch. When fishing the Tay, the Minister and I were accustomed to success, to be acknowledged of course with seemly modesty. Great Gran, five feet tall, made us feel small that day.

Four years ago, Gran had a ducking in icy water while wading the Tweed in the early spring. She needed a bit of help before getting thawed out in the fishing hut; and then carried on fishing. She now boasts that her frost-bitten fingers provide signals of changes in the weather. Highland women of her generation seem tough in strength and spirit. When autumn fish are filling the Earn, I hope to help her to increase her score.

Bats on the bob fly

For many years my tallest true fishing story was the one about simultaneously playing the salmon, sea trout and brown trout that evening on the Inver. Surprisingly, the proximity of the small fish thrashing the surface did not make that stately September salmon move any faster. I later had an experience which I found even more surprising – simultaneously playing a large seatrout and a bat. My surprise, however, was nothing compared with that of the fish. This is how it happened.

I had a week at the end of June on unfamiliar water, Tulchan on the Spey. By Tuesday evening it had become clear that salmon were very scarce. I had, however, seen a couple of large sea trout lunging in a glide close to the trees at the tail of a long pool. I went out that evening to try for them. I had not, as I should have done, explored the wading while there was light enough to see. Getting to the right place by the direct route turned out to be tricky. It involved negotiating fifty yards of fast boulder-strewn river before I could get within casting distance of the trees on the opposite bank. Several times I nearly lost my balance in water over three feet deep. Before I had got out a full casting line I hooked a fish, which, after a heavy pull, behaved disconcertingly. It let me wind in all my line and proceeded to bore directly under the tip of my nine foot rod, apparently regarding my stationary self as another tree. I unfolded my net, confident that the pressure that I was giving it would bring it to the surface fairly soon.

As the minutes passed I grew impatient. After ten minutes, I was debating whether the fish was big enough to warrant the very unwelcome wade back to my home bank. Then a bat took and got hooked on the dropper fly and momentarily fluttered a few inches above the water. The fish went off like a bat out of hell. After a long run, it proceeded to do aerial acrobatics for half a minute. It was too dark to see the display, but the splashes resounded across the river. Then suddenly peace was restored. The fish came quietly to heel and continued boring around my legs. The bat had gone.

It was now clear that the fish was *well* over five pounds and must be beached, not netted. So back I went, groping with my feet, with the fish never more than four yards away, until I had almost reached the bank. Then, of course, the fish was averse to leave the current and enter the slack water in which I stood. When at last I had got it into calm water and caught a glimpse of its big silver flank, I was sure it was mine. If only I had remembered the torch in my pocket and held it between my teeth, I might have netted it. But while it was still resisting attempts to force it these last few yards to the shingle, guess what happened. Another damned bat committed suicide by taking the bob fly! I fear that at this point some readers are going to doubt my veracity. I have never heard of anyone hooking a bat *while* playing a fish. To have this happen twice with the same fish is an incredible coincidence. The effect on the fish was as electrifying as it had been the first time. It did a thirty yard sprint wriggling through the surface of the river and then dived. I was half-way through pulling it back when the hook came unstuck. This bat too had gone. It may, of course, have survived the water-skiing.

If anyone wishes to try to repeat this experience, I might add that my dropper fly was a No. 8 Butcher – too big, I would have thought, for hooking bats. But he may have to wait a lifetime before meeting a seatrout which behaves as mine did and leaves the dropper dangling, almost stationary, for minutes on end. I have never known another seatrout behave like this. Perhaps it was a salmon. Conceivably it was hooked in a pectoral fin, though this seems unlikely since I was using a floating line and light trout flies. I do not recommend attempts to repeat the experiment. You have my testimony about that fish's reaction to bats; and those harmless creatures do not deserve such a fright, and, I fear, a watery end.

A red-letter day

I knew from friends that Esmond Drury's flies, especially the Stoat's Tail, had been strikingly successful in other rivers, including the Dee and the Spey. I decided in 1972 to try them on the Tay. It is not fair to generalise from a one-day trial, but, using them, I wasted what could have been a red-letter Monday on Upper Stobhall. Above, on Islamouth, a limit catch of twenty fish was being caught on fly. Meanwhile I was being teased in the Alderns and Stankend by as many salmon, which broke the surface to inspect my No. 10 Stoat's Tail; almost always without touching it, *or* the No. 12, *or* No. 8, which I then systematically offered to them. Three of these fish were felt, but only one grilse was landed. One came unstuck after a few seconds and one broke the hook after five minutes (or had I already broken one of its three hooks?)

That evening I reverted to my fail-me-never – the Hairy Mary dressed with red buck-tail on Low Water double-hooks. I caught a fish and lost another after a long battle. For the rest of the week I stuck to these flies with happy results. Not once did I see a fish move to my fly without its taking hold. The fish proved to be not at all fussy about the size of the fly. Numbers 8 and 10 were equally successful in the day-time, and sizes 1, 4 and 10 were taken in the evening. And these flies gave me, on Wednesday, the red-letter day which I thought I had missed: ten fish weighing 100 pounds from eleven offers.

The grilse which had passed Perth during the week-end slap were still travelling through, fat fish of six to nine pounds which fought in the fast water like fish of twice their weight. The sport was not continuous. There was nearly an hour of casting between each fish, but my score mounted up, and by tea-time it was seven weighing fifty-four pounds. After an early dinner, I returned to fish the gloaming hour. This can be profitable if the air is still warm. My optimism dwindled, however, when chilly rain started to fall on my arrival, and with low clouds the light was departing too soon.

Unexpectedly, it was one of those evenings when you waste little time casting. Indeed the first fish took hold *before* my first cast – while I lit a cigarette at the top of the Alderns, with two yards of line trailing by the edge of the stream. I played that strong salmon with care and caution, as I had lost the only big one so far hooked that week. It turned out to be a silvery eighteen pounder, hooked on a Butcher (the trout fly) used on the dropper. About one minute later my rod was bending again. I was hard on this fish, because I was now aiming at breaking my personal record by catching ten salmon in a day, and it was almost too dark to hope for another offer. A thirteen pounder was soon beached.

I started again a few yards below the place where I had hooked the other fish and pulled twenty yards of line off the reel before making my first cast. Incredibly, I hooked another with my second cast. This fish raced towards the sea, and I stumbled down-stream trying to keep up with it. When I got level with it, all of my fly line was spread, vibrating, across the strong current. Then the fish changed its tactics and ran up-stream on the far side of the main current right up into the thin water. Almost inevitably there came that dead strain which means that the line is round a boulder. For several minutes I waded up and then down pulling from different angles, but the strain stayed dead. In this same place and predicament Jim had once lost a new fly line. I had resigned myself to the same fate and was about to pull to breaking point, when the light dawned on my fatigue-dimmed wits. My line was pointing 45° up-stream and the fish was surely *above* the offending boulder. Since my line was a floater, with luck all I need do to release it was to let out backing until the line stretched straight below that boulder. It worked. In almost pitch darkness, I beached a thick fresh-run fish of fifteen pounds. If days like this were at all common, I think I *might* get bored with salmon fishing. As if to renew the challenge, I caught nothing on the Friday on Upper Stobhall, while George Mann wiped my eye by catching three weighty fish.

When I sent to *Trout and Salmon* the above account of that day, I sent a copy to Colonel Drury whose flies I had criticised prematurely. I received by return a letter which sounded rather aggrieved. It contained some justified rejoinders, and also said that he had formed the impression that I was 'an enthusiastic angler of very limited experience who has the good fortune to fish a very good beat'. I naturally asked the editor to delete the words which had given offence, and since then, Colonel Drury and I have become pen-friends. As he knows, I soon became a convert to his flies. And he, after fishing Islamouth, has confirmed my own experience – that his smallest hooks, sizes 10 and 12, are liable to tear out in prolonged fights, when fish have the help of the Tay's water power. Now that his flies are so deservedly popular, I am sure that he will not mind my saying that I find that *in the Tay* Low Water double irons get a better grip when you have to fish with flies of the smallest sizes.

Opportunities missed

It was the last day on which I would be free to fish during my first season in North Wales. On my three or four ticket days on the Gwydyr Hotel water, I had not yet met the salmon really in the mood. 'You need a big flood', the locals said. This should be it, as the overnight rain had been heavy. Too heavy, I thought, when the Conway came into sight. It was up to the flood banks and looked like lentil soup. I could see at a glance that the pools I knew would be unfishable, and set out to explore. What I was looking for was the inside bend of a pool where resident fish as well as runners would seek haven under the bank. I found what I was looking for – Hafod. I did not then know its name, nor how many of the huge seatrout which homed to the Conway in the late 1950s settled there.

That morning the snag was that I could fish only the top fifty yards of the pool. Trees with boughs awash would prevent my following, or perhaps snag, a hooked fish. The morning was monotonous, repeatedly going over the little stretch with a big copper and silver spoon, a good old spoon-shaped spoon. If need be, you can make an all silver one out of a kitchen spoon and fish will not discriminate against it. I had learned elsewhere that such spoons attract fish in water too coloured for anything else to be seen (or perhaps it is the spoon's vibrations which are felt?). I was not discouraged by lunchtime. It had been worming water, but now it was falling quite fast. I saw no point in moving elsewhere, since the fish would be doing the moving. Often in such conditions there is only an hour or so of the fireworks, and one does not want to be walking the bank when that starts. To encourage me a big fellow showed at my feet. I postponed finishing the sandwich. Back to work. Half-way down my tiny beat, the spoon was seized close to the bank. The fish was 100 yards down and across before it stopped to draw oxygen, and my fingers were skinned by using them as a brake. When spinning, I am not in the habit of using the slipping clutch and this time, anyway, I would have had no time to slacken the tension.

For ten minutes it was pull devil pull baker, for if it got a little nearer to the tail of the pool there would be no stopping it. I had managed to walk it up a few yards, then: Twang – I had lost twenty yards of nylon. I did not change to another drum of line as only short casting was needed. I brooded as I continued to fish. *Was* I pulling too hard? Surely not. My rod had remained where I could kiss it without bending, and the thirteen-pound nylon was almost new. My spirits revived as more and more fish showed about ten yards out. Momentarily my spirits soared again. I had just changed to a big red and gold devon, as autumn salmon, like Spanish bulls, seem readily provoked by red. But after a heavy pull, a big fish surfaced, waved a lazy tail, and the hold gave. I returned to the sandwich tin and very belatedly finished lunch.

I knew that I would slog on until dark and still had about four hours – time for half a dozen, but my confidence had been undermined. I fished mechanically. The hours passed slowly. Around 7 p.m. a series of anglers passed me by, heading towards hotel and dinner. None had touched a fish. I was tempted to join the procession, but an hour of fishing light remained – the last of my season. I reverted to using a spoon if only to revive my hopes. I chose a massive triangular solid copper spoon. Mallochs had found two of them in a dusty corner, made for Mahseer, they thought. They looked genuine antiques. Its twin had done well on the Tay; two large salmon in about ten casts, then irretrievably stuck at the next cast – a present for some future pearl fisher.

Whether it was the 'vibes' from the spoon, or from me, the response was instantaneous, and this fish behaved in a most eccentric manner, like a ball in play at Wimbledon. It consumed its energy so fast that I had it ashore within five minutes. It came in tail first, but not foul-hooked; indeed not hooked at all, but lassooed round the wrist of its tail! It was a nerve-racking five minutes, for when you have had a few losses, you fear the worst. It was, incidentally, a thirteen-pound seatrout. It was now gloaming, and the fish were really on. The next was not on for long, however, and it kept the antique spoon. My line parted when the fish was merely leaning on the current. So I felt the last ten yards of line. It seemed a little rough, so I removed it. Back to the red and gold, and only three casts later I was into a monster. I knew from the way it shook its head and its slow relentless movements.

I fought with that fish for an hour and three quarters. I gave it more butt than I have ever given a fish. It made not the slightest impression. It played me, at its leisure. It never *ran*. It alternated between ten minute rests (chewing the hook?) and ten minute walks, so to speak. I could feel the slow beat of its tail when *it* walked *me* downstream. I had filled my waders getting round those trees when it chose to leave Hafod. By then it was pitch dark. No moon, thick cloud and my torch was back in my bag. It took me nearly a mile down-stream, by easy stages; easy for it, that is, not for me as I had never seen the banks, bushes or fences. My right arm was about to drop off. I felt more relief than sorrow when the hook broke. I had known for some time that it was hopeless as we were nearing a railway bridge, beyond which I could not follow its seaward course. I felt relief, though of course I would never have parted company deliberately. Still, I had been spared another half-hour of vain struggle. Fortunately I was the first predator to find my seatrout. Others might have found it by scent. I had to locate it by a bump of direction and a sense of touch.

When a hook breaks I blame the maker. When my line breaks I blame myself. I was certainly right to do so this time. Next day, I found some slight scratches on its surface. Then I remembered the cause. Two months earlier when last I used this line, I had cracked the agate end-ring of another spinning rod and used it for another hour. I had, at the end of that day, stupidly removed only the few yards of new line which were obviously scratched. It was the same line that I had used on the Conway, with damage which I had not noticed. I had lost two good fish through culpable negligence. That finished me for life with agate rings. Has anyone ever lost fish through using the cheaper metal end-rings?

Nearly drowned

When wading I do occasionally fall in. There is, of course, no malice in the story that I dripped back to Dess House *thrice* in one day, to shed my wet clothing and return at once to the river. Whose memory is infallible? I know, however, that I returned to change only twice. I had only brought two pairs of breast waders. Admittedly I also filled the thigh boots used later in the day, but that did not interrupt my fishing as the last slippage occurred when playing an evening fish. Forgetful about many things, encounters with salmon are imprinted indelibly upon my memory. When fishing less close to a wardrobe, I normally keep in the car some 'falling in' clothes. It is when I fail to take these that I have another ducking. Only one of these was a serious matter.

It was when Jim and I had just joined the summer free fishers and were exploring the lower Tay. We had not yet learned that Islamouth was taboo, because it was sometimes let during the dog-days. (Nowadays, I believe, it is let every day of the season.) We had not seen a boat on it, as we ventured only a little above the Cargill Viaduct, where we found enough to keep us busy without more walking. The water was unexpectedly high on the afternoon in question, and the end of the big groyne 200 yards above the viaduct was awash. I tentatively waded too far along it. Water sucked fiercely at my wading brogues. Turning round cautiously to return, I slipped. Suddenly the world was cold, wet and confusing.

The week before the local papers had headlined the sad account of an angler drowned in the Tay; and of course I had read the horror stories about what happens to people who fall in while wearing breast waders – the air in your waders keeps your feet up and your head down. Fortunately it didn't happen to me. When I had got orientated, and some air back in my lungs, I found to my relief that I could, after a fashion, swim – a sort of back stroke. Though that description is misleading in suggesting that I was horizontal. At best I was only half-way towards the horizontal, due to the weight of my wading brogues. But I was, thank God, making some slow progress through the water. My heart beat more slowly – all was well. I found that I was still clutching my rod. This did not aid swimming, but why waste a good rod? It was at most twenty-five yards to the shore.

Several times I stopped swimming, expecting to find my feet on rock, and each time sank. So far I had watched the sky, keeping calm.

I made an effort to look over my shoulder, and got a glimpse of Jim in the distance standing gawping at me, and of the place where I had fallen in *about ten yards straight up-stream*. I panicked, conscious of my fatigue, let go my rod, redoubled my efforts. Efforts, efforts . . . until I knew I had used up all my energy. Either I was now within my depth or I'd had it. (No pictures of my past life passed before my blank mind.) I let my feet go down. They met the bottom several seconds *after* the world had disappeared. But the feel of terra firma stimulated one more kick and a few weak arm strokes. This time I came to rest with my nose just above the water. I do not know how long I stood there while fatigue and fear drained away. In due course, I dragged myself ashore and threw myself upon that lovely grass.

When I sat up, Jim had been talking for some time but I had not taken in a word. I then exploded (weakly): 'Why the hell didn't you do something?' 'What could I do? You know I can't swim.' 'You could have hooked me from the croy, and helped to tow me in.' 'But I might have hooked you in the face.' 'Better defaced than dead.' (That last line is too neat to be accurate, but it is the gist of what I said.)

I struggled to my feet and surveyed the water where I had been struggling for dear life. I had been swimming straight into the back-water, and in the deep hole which had been formed by, and below, that down-stream slanting croy. That is why my initial motion relative to the water had left me motionless relative to the bank. Jim, chastened by my long silence, said at last: 'Didn't you hear me shouting "Swim downstream"?' I hadn't, with the noise of the river and my ears waterlogged. It would have been so simple. A few strokes out into the stream, a little float and I would have been down on the shingle where we had waded earlier when fishing. Since then I never wade where I think drowning *possible*, without deciding in advance how to get out should I have to swim.

I did not lose that rod. The salvage operation involved fitting a pane of glass in the bottom of a biscuit tin, the pearl fisher's method of seeing the river bed in those pre-Polaroid days. Next day I launched myself in bathing trunks on a Lilo, located the rod and retrieved it with a long gaff made longer with a spare broom handle.

Nearly eaten alive?

After spending four months teaching in an American university near the Atlantic, I spent a week driving west in early June aiming towards Vancouver. I had brought only some trout tackle. I was lucky to choose April Point Lodge for the three days available for catching my first Pacific salmon. It was the most hospitable fishing hostelry that I found in British Columbia. It was geared for the travelling angler whose salmon tackle and oilskins are in another continent. From the dining-room one watched porpoises and seals a stone's throw away. My third morning there was a gem. The clouds had gone and the snow-clad peaks of Vancouver Island shimmered in the west beyond Campbell River. As we left the jetty a bald eagle sailed over us, trailing a rock-cod, and we paused to watch the young eagle climb the nest edge to receive its breakfast. Then Warren Peterson, my amiable 'guide', drove his fibreglass boat at full throttle up Discovery Passage. We hit a log in the choppy water, but luckily sprang no leak. We halted in the Narrows, six miles north. Here the Sound is only about half a mile wide and the ebbing tide was pouring through it at over twenty knots. Today I felt confident of catching a 'spring' (a Chinook salmon). The last two mornings I had failed, despite opportunities. Twice a fish had come unstuck after long and powerful runs. I had indeed played and landed four lively Coho salmon of about five pounds each and a twenty-three pound Spring, though they were not really *my* fish but Warren's, for all had been hooked on the troll.

Fishing in the Narrows is very different. When the tide is running hard, it is like an enormous river. The only fishable water is about forty by eighty yards of churning back-waters and ever-changing whirlpools. Here, betwixt tide-race and rocky shore, millions of herring-fry get temporarily trapped, an easy meal for salmon. My problem had been to interpret plucks and twitches and decide when to strike. No doubt my ineptitude, with unfamiliar tackle and methods, was responsible for at least some of the occasions when my bait had vanished from the hooks or come back torn. The bait was a herring of five or six inches, on two single hooks, mounted whole to give a slow spin, or sometimes with head and belly sliced off to spin more rapidly. Four ounces of lead were used to get it deep enough. Once the line was out, it was Warren, by controlling the boat, who determined where and how the bait was moving, but at least I had to strike when I had an offer. Usually the offers came when the bait was moving from faster to slower water at a depth of ten to fifteen yards.

Today, standing in the stern, I concentrated hard on watching my rod tip and fingering the line on the borrowed Silex reel. I had decided to strike on the first sign of an offer. Attempts to carry out my earlier instructions, to wait for a second and more decisive pull, had not worked. I did not have long to wait. My prompt strike was into something very solid, which ran fast and far out into the tide-race, and had nearly two hundred yards' start before Warren could keep pace with it. In relation to the land, we had covered well over a mile in two minutes before the fish started to slacken its speed. There was an anxious minute as a steamer bound for Alaska swept down-stream, heading for a point between us and the fish. Disaster was averted just in time by the fish going deep. The later stages of the fight were in less turbulent water with the fish boring, sometimes a hundred yards below us. When Warren had finally netted this short, thick, twenty-pound spring, his delight was as unconcealed as mine.

In a few minutes his powerful motor had us back in the fishing area, now shared with another boat from April Point. On the previous morning both boats had fished here, and three times I had watched the other boat going off down-tide in pursuit of a big spring, and returning with victory signals. Our purely spectators' role had probably tried Warren's patience more than mine, since the youthful guide in the other boat was his understudy. But today my turn had come. Within the next hour the drama was repeated twice, and we had two more springs aboard, each of eighteen pounds. Meanwhile the other boat was reporting that fish were pecking without taking their baits. Fortune changed favours as the tide eased off, and the other boat ended the morning with two springs, bigger than ours. All I achieved from a further half-dozen offers was a five-pounder, which I spared in the hope of catching another big one to complete my limit of four for the day.

For me the grand climax of the morning, indeed of the holiday, came just after the netting of my third fish – the breath-taking spectacle of a dozen killer-whales advancing line abreast up the Sound, the nearest of them about two hundred and fifty yards away. Usually they slid out of the water dolphin style, but sometimes one pushed its head up towards the sky, revealing its white chest and grinning mouth before subsiding vertically. 'Please let's take a closer look' was my immediate request, but Warren's urgent concern was to divert them from our fishing ground for which they were heading. They eat salmon as well as seals, etc. With no delay he did two circuits at full speed round the water they had just been disturbing. Successfully, for a minute later we saw them crossing to the other side of the Narrows. Warren was so self-confident that it was only later that I wondered if one could *rely* upon killer-whales to take evasive action when attacked by a boat of a third of their length. Otherwise Warren may long since have become whale meat.

The stay at April Point was a delight for many reasons. One was the uninhibited affection among the Peterson family. Warren, a tough, bold, forty-year-old ex-Marine, was always addressed by his father as 'my dear' – even when his dear son said: 'Daddy, you'll have to get me a new boat. I guess I hit another log'. And they kindly canned my catch, so that many Americans whose hospitality I had enjoyed received cans of smoked salmon with my name on the label.

Anglers arriving in British Columbia can, I found, get invaluable help in planning a fishing holiday by consulting the B.C. Travel Bureau in Vancouver, Victoria or Banff. Each office receives, weekly, fairly detailed reports about the fishing results from the main angling centres. I was briefed at Banff about the current catches in lakes near Kamloops, and by visiting some of them, *en route* for April Point, I enjoyed more than one splendid evening rise. During the best, my catch – nine trout weighing twelve pounds in about an hour – might have been doubled, if I had not got a bird's nest of a tangle and forgotten a torch *and* a spare cast. I was warned by the travel bureau that in June the chances of catching salmon in the sea are problematical. Pacific salmon do not start to enter fresh water till early autumn, and the peak of the seafishing season is in August and September. I would gladly settle for June again. The trout fishing is at its best, and though the salmon are then less numerous, so too are the anglers.

Jim's tangle

There were two tangles if I may exploit the ambiguity of this word. The unresolved one will come at the end. Eleven months earlier, P had promised me *in writing* the last week on Stobhall before the nets came off. Jim and I, and our families, had made plans accordingly. I had sent P's letter to Jim, who swore that he had returned it, but he hadn't. He found it when it was only of historical interest. Shortly before the big week was to start, I dropped in to pay P. Both times I got a glimpse of him hastily disappearing into his office and was then told that he was out. The second time, I asked what was going on and made to follow P into his office. My way was barred by a very embarrassed assistant who then came clean – P had forgotten his promise, had let Stobhall to a Duke, and nothing could be done!

Jim ransacked his house for the letter without success. We felt anger and despair. But that evening at a party, Jim made friends with a Procurator-Fiscal, and he too was an angler. 'Come and see me tomorrow morning when I've sobered up', he said. We visited him together not too early, on Saturday morning. In case some readers do not know our Scottish legal system, Procurator-Fiscals are men whom one is careful not to cross, or make cross. It is they who decide whether to prosecute, but the good ones sort out many a tangle without resort to the Courts. His 'phone call to P was terse: 'I hear what you've done to Professor Mundle. I won't have this sort of thing in my bailiwick. Please 'phone me back within fifteen minutes and confirm his fishing arrangements.' I was surprised at the tough line he took when he had not seen the letter. Fortunately Scottish anglers trust each other. Ten minutes later the 'phone rang and we were offered a compromise. We had no choice but to accept it, for it seemed reasonable to our legal protagonist; who did not appreciate that at this season few fish stopped running until they had passed Campsie Lynn. The Duke and the Mundles would each get three days on Stobhall and a boat would be laid on specially on a lower beat, Upper Scone, to give the Mundles the rest of their week.

It was the sort of week to cure, if that were possible, the most addicted angler. What P had promised me was bank fishing and the use of boats to cross the river. On both beats we met two boatmen, strangers to us, and they did not wish to use the boat to fish for us. We felt morally obliged to take turns at sitting in the boat, in the deluge which went on all week. The river alternated between Bovril-coloured floods and white coffee cataracts. The black clouds met the trees. My week's catch was one small grilse, and it was scarcely my catch, though I wound it in when it took on the harl in the famous, enormous, Pitlochry Pool. There must have been fish running all week, but they never showed. On the last afternoon (of a Bovril day) I was really cross with Jim. He did not turn up at lunch to release me from the boat.

That night I received his apologies, and his explanation. He had fished his way down the left bank of Upper Scone, and just before lunch-time reached the inner curve of Tail of Horsey Pool – tailor-made for running fish to pause in after a stretch of very strong water. He caught a grilse at last, and then could not tear himself away. I understood. He fished on hungry through the afternoon and lost two or three fish on big spoons. (These are not efficient in hooking, unless you replace the maker's huge triangles with ones much smaller.) Jim then displayed to me his twenty-pounder and the very mysterious tangle which he had found when he got it ashore. He had cut his nylon above the tangle and left the spoon in place, for me to explain the puzzle. It looked like this:

The knots in the bird's nest tangle were pulled too tight for unpicking; an activity which would have explained nothing. The puzzle was the disappearance of the swivel and the fold-over anti-kink lead. Sticking out from the tangle were two pieces of nylon which had linked with these missing objects, and they bore no signs of chafing. Had Jim been a less experienced angler, I told him, I'd assume, despite his assurances to the contrary, that he must have twisted his line and made a sloppy cast, that, before the spoon was working, the nylon between swivel and spoon somehow formed a tangle with the nylon above the swivel; and that at some stage in the prolonged fight, the heavy lead, dangling down, had caught between rocks and got broken off. But Jim swore that the fish had been under continuous hard pressure throughout the fight and at no point had the line been fouled on a rock. I am sure *he* would have known if it was, and he did not make sloppy casts.

I remain baffled. My foregoing tentative explanation was, on second thoughts, not credible. Suppose that it had happened as I had (offensively) surmised – when the lead or swivel was jammed between rocks, what would break? Surely it would have been the single strand above or below the tangle, not *both* strands of the loop, whose breaking strain was thereby doubled; for presumably we should have to suppose that each strand of the loop broke simultaneously – thc breaking of one strand would simply have released the fish from the hypothetical snag. Can anyone else explain? An open cut-throat razor being swept down in mid-water by the flood?

A salmon lie narrowly avoided

Thelwell has illustrated the relevant kind of salmon lie (*Compleat Tangler*, p. 109): an irate keeper clutches by the neck an embarrassed man trying to explain the presence of the salmon lying at their feet.

The fate which I narrowly avoided is described in the Badminton Library thus: 'A poacher . . . and his wife and children are clothed in rags; his idleness and loafing habits are habitual to him, for he will not accept honest well-paid work . . . He cannot run – he is too heavy and bloated with drink to do so.' (*Shooting: Field and Covert*, p. 300). I do not myself think these generalisations are valid for *all* parts of this kingdom. I fear, however, that if the authors of that book could read the following (hi)story, they would concede at most that I am an exception who proves their rules.

This episode still pricks my conscience. It happened during the first season when Jim and I regarded ourselves as salmon fishers, though we were still equally addicted to the trout. I took Jim to Lochinver to introduce him to trout lochs which I had discovered while he was adventuring around Vancouver. The hotel was full, but we found homely accommodation on the other side of the Inver bridge. We learned much during that week about the Highlanders' attitudes towards an absentee landlord – especially from the cheerful lad on the Inver bridge, who was, like us, ex-RAF. He needed no prompting to recount gleefully some of his poaching exploits. We could not wait to hear all of them, as we wanted a little fishing. Daily, he *said*, he followed the tenants down the Inver pools, keeping just out of sight of them, catching more on worm than they did on fly. Apparently it was not only in the hotel that salmon was on the menu.

On our last day, I persuaded Jim to endure the longish walk up the glen of the Kirkaig to Loch Fionn. I had good memories of it, apart from the views of Suilven. There, after a week of coaching, Sheila had caught a pounder on a Blue Zulu. It was a triumph for me at the time, but when, later, she said 'What's the point?', I knew that her angling career had no future. (Jim's wife caught a salmon before going on strike.) Half a mile out of Lochinver, we stopped the car to find what occupied the crowd of men and boys by the pools of a small stream. A baptism? A pagan ritual? No – they were merely spearing and gaffing a run of salmon ascending to the lochan. We recognised the lad we had met on the bridge, and drove on. We had a disappointing day on Fionn – a dozen, only three to the pound, some of them from the lazy river below its exit from the loch. Walking back, at about 6 p.m., I took Jim down to see the spectacular Falls Pool, unpassable by salmon.

Now Jim was rather a devil-may-care, which was not surprising after surviving fifty Bomber missions and so many of the crews with whom he had flown. Our mother had had more success in moulding my inhibitions. He dared me to have a cast for a salmon. I succumbed, not taking seriously the possibility of success. We had with us a trout spinning rod which we had not used that day. The nearest we had to a salmon lure was a one-inch Vibro spoon. It was the work of two minutes to cover the tail of the pool – the only part fishable by fly fishers. Having met Jim's challenge, I was about to dismantle the rod, when a salmon showed in the cauldron above. It was now the fish's challenge which got me. Miraculously, I caught it. The miracle was not in hooking it but in landing it. An angler here must stand on a few square feet of natural rock four or five feet above the water. Vertically below this is a tiny ledge then less than a foot above the black torrent which would carry you out of the pool, bashing you on rocks, if you fell in. From this ledge a ghillie has to gaff an angler's fish. Had my fish got below this point, it would have been impossible to pull it back on my five-pound nylon line. This fish committed suicide. It wore itself out in the depths below the waterfall, until, lying on its side, it let me draw it down the near edge of the cauldron. Jim, risking his life as he bent precariously down, got his fingers in its gills as it passed. With his left hand clutching the rock where my feet rested, he slowly passed it up to me. A fourteen pounder! We lost no time in tucking it into my rucksack which then displayed a most conspicuous U-shaped bulge. We emptied the last Thermos to calm our nerves, and set off down the path.

At the crest of a hillock we found ourselves face to face with M, the hotel manager, not wearing his usual smile, and a still more unsmiling man, introduced to us as the Estate Factor. With some embarrassment M explained that a guest returning from Fionn had reported two strangers fishing the river. 'That must have been us', I said, 'we found the loch so dour that we tried the part where it becomes a river.' Jim added: 'If you think we're after salmon, look at our tackle.' Matching deeds to his words, he took from their cases our two fly rods and the flimsy spinning rod. (They were not to know that the bend in the latter had been so recently acquired.) Having so clearly established that we were not *armed* for salmon, we walked back together. Occasional attempts at chat by Jim and myself ended in rather uneasy silences.

I had forgotten how many damned gates there were on the lower part of the path; and at every gate I had to play the 'after you' game. At the first few it could have been my natural politeness. By the time we got to my car they must surely have noticed signs of the weight of my rucksack, and have guessed why I never let them get behind me. Fortunately their car was a little down-stream from mine. After manifest hesitation, they left us there. With the rucksack thrown on the back seat, I trod on the accelerator. Half-way to Lochinver, Jim reported their car driving fast a furlong behind. Panic – of course we could be trapped if they drew up behind us at our homely digs, and kept guard until a policeman arrived. Jim's head was cooler than mine. He got the salmon out of the sack, told me to slow down while crossing a little burn, opened the car door and deftly threw the fish into some thick heather. We were speeding on when the following car reappeared in my mirror.

They did not, after all, follow us beyond the hotel. I suppose they did not fancy keeping guard until a PC arrived, from Inverness.

When we reached the Inver bridge, the happy lad was there again. Now fellow poachers, we stopped to tell *our* tale. When, at last, he had stopped laughing, he said: 'We must'na let a goot fish rot – chust tell me just where it is.' He went back and retrieved it! Later he called on us to hand it over, but we insisted on his keeping it 'for the poor of the parish.' We knew they were not short of salmon, but I had to try to salve my conscience.

What nagged it, still does, is that M was no stranger. When I had been a guest in his hotel, he, a kind host and a fellow angler, had gone out of his way to advise me how and where to fill my creel. I had put him in a most embarrassing situation. Should he read this, I beg his pardon. I am sure that my confession will not surprise him. I am no actor. I could not have been convincing doing that 'After you, Claude' act at *so* many gates.

Spey casting

As you will doubtless know, Spey casting is *one* of the ways of throwing a fly a long way when there are trees or a high bank close behind you. As performed by my would-be teachers it involves 'aerialising' a lot of line in a figure of eight. The line splashes out across the river via up-stream and then down-stream coils. It seems well adapted for developing muscles. Nevertheless three lessons in this art cured me of any desire for a fourth. Performed by an expert it is a *tour de force* of control of rod and line, an art to be cultivated for Art's sake, or for prestige. But given the relative simplicity of roll casting, I have found it unnecessary to combine it with the art of fly fishing.

My first lesson was impromptu, on a June evening at Grantown when, unusually, the salmon showing were nearly as numerous as the anglers. One of the Masters was resting after doing his thing. I said: 'Please show me how.' If only he had used his larger rod and not my twelve-foot Grant. He had about thirty yards out, on his way to forty, when there was a distinct crack. He heard it too, wound in and said 'Now you try.' The butt of the best Greenheart rod that I ever owned had to be replaced. It was never the same rod. Waddington was right when he wrote that such rods, made to identical specifications, vary widely in both action and power.

Lesson Two. A real enthusiast from Grantown promised to take me to a rather inaccessible pool (a) because it was the best for miles around for seatrout at dusk, (b) to teach me to Spey cast. To leave time for (b), we got there before the sun was off the water. He was evidently a one-rod man, and it was evidently his grandfather's twenty footer. The lesson was to have been conducted above the superb seatrout pool. Unfortunately a few salmon were showing in the latter near the far bank, so it was: 'Hang on a moment till I show them a Jock Scott.' I was then forgotten. It was indeed a spectacle as he waded the gravel from which seatrout must have been fleeing. Never before have I seen a line raise such waves and spray as it rolled out across the forty yards of calm water to the distant rough. The pool was long as well as wide. Some stars were visible when at last he rejoined me. So it was: 'Sorry, I had a pull. Too late for the lesson now. It's seatrout time. Just you fish the lower half down where I've been fishing, and I'll try a pool up above!' I suspected then what I know now – that the seatrout would have taken hours to recover from the repeated thrashing of their homes with that cable of a line.

No-one who has fished and watched fish in clear water in little streams like Ogwen, Lledr or Ailort, would dream of fishing for seatrout in smooth water until the bats have been out for some time. They would have observed that the shadow of a passing bird will make these fish leave their lies, and that salmon are nearly as shy of strange movements, shadows, and thick lines; never mind boats with outboard motors! I used to decline the use of the boat when fishing Cargill, though from it I could have shown flies to salmon out of wading range. Once was enough. That boatman raced his outboard motor up the middle of the salmon lies, anchored it and said: 'Carry on – they are down below you.' They *had been*. Big river specialists cannot see what goes on beneath the surface.

Lesson Three. The day on Tulchan had started ill for our soft-spoken, Highland ghillie. The fishing hut had been broken into overnight and his rods and tackle had gone. Sunbathing at the end of our picnic lunch, I idly asked him to demonstrate the Spey cast. He was delighted to oblige and fetched his only remaining rod, a fourteen-foot spliced Sharpe, fortunately kept in his car overnight. He did it beautifully. Between each cast he tore another three or four yards from the reel. I had never seen so much line coiling through a figure of eight. Would he stop before hooking the other bank? He did. With an almighty crack his rod broke cleanly in the middle. Had I been in his shoes, my feelings would have boiled over. He had more self control. He slowly turned, waded ashore and said, with a wry smile: 'It's no' my day.' Happily, as he told me next summer, the police later retrieved his other rods, hidden near a gypsy encampment. I assume that Spey casters work on the principle of *aggravating* salmon as illustrated by Thelwell opposite.

Arthur Oglesby assures me that a Spey cast need not be a Splash cast. I had wasted his time by asking him to make for me a photograph of the figure of eight. This is impossible for a reason which I had overlooked. If a camera is to record a sharp image of the moving line, the exposure time must be 1/200th of a second or less. Our eyes are more ingenious. When we watch moving objects (a line, a ball, a Catherine wheel) we *see* the object continuously in the positions which it has occupied throughout the previous tenth of a second or more. Only a specialised cine-camera could capture the

SALMON DO NOT FEED IN FRESH WATER
SO THE ANGLER'S ONLY HOPE
IS TO AGGRAVATE THEM

desired effect.

River improvements

I had not foreseen getting stuck with so much work. Nor could the Club committee have foreseen all that they were putting on my plate when they asked me to supervise the construction of a new pool on the Ogwen and the repair of an old one. No-one else had volunteered. In a sense I had asked for it. I had urged the Club to ask the River Board for such aid. I was hoping that it would be given freely, as it had been on the neighbouring River Seiont. This now had a whole mile of new pools, rather crudely constructed with a drag-line excavator. Some of the weirs looked vulnerable to floods. Still, a few visits there had given me a couple of early (May) salmon, and I had got there rather late, about 7 a.m. – one of the latest of the early birds.

The Seiont Club, unlike ours, had no limit to its membership. That is why it got free service. I know not whether the River Board employed a clairvoyant, but their estimate for what it would cost us was *very* close to the sum which our Club had then accumulated. I was not very keen on the assignment, as I knew I would get all the blame for wasting our hard-earned savings if things went wrong. I had studied two or three books devoted to River Improvements, but I need not have bothered. About all that had been agreed therein was that those wealthy Victorians had made a bloomer in building croys, big and small, *all* slanting down-stream, like the one which nearly drowned me. This causes bank erosion below the croys (as well as nasty deep holes and backwaters). Modern croys slant up-stream. More about river improvement can, however, be learnt from passing discussions in books by some who own, love and groom the water they fish; e.g. Mrs. Robertson's slice of the Slaney, L.R.N. Gray's stretch of the Torridge.

It was worth trying anyway. Our two best pools for seatrout, and for salmon in high water, were man-made, presumably by the first Baron of Penrhyn. The weirs had been skilfully constructed. They sloped down-stream at about 45°, composed of cobbles neatly fitted together. The biggest of these pools, 'Gordon's', was still intact. The second, 'the Mill' had a slipping weir, and this process would accelerate unless something was done soon. My main interest was in what was still *called* a pool, the 'Long Pool', but was now little more than a potential; except for the top few bouldery yards, where before the river fell from flood to burn level, it could detain a salmon.

Fortunately for me the drag-line excavator arrived just after my external examiner left, and I had two more weeks of rainless June before the seatrout really started to run. It was as well that I was free every morning and afternoon, as the operator had used his machine only to make or deepen ditches, and knew as much about running water and its fauna as an inhabitant of Mars. At first I could scarcely turn my back without his doing something that had to be undone. He was, however, cheerful, energetic and keen to please; and when I met him later, he could have earned much more than I did, if he had sold his skill in making fishing pools to those who value them. It was trial and error for both of us. I had to learn from scratch what could and could not be done with the help of this machine. He had to learn what we, and the fish, wanted. I had to try to get the plan right at the first guess, as extra time would mean extra cost and an overdraft for the Club.

What the new Long Pool needed was a weir which would raise the level by about three feet, with the low water outlet under the high, tree-lined, right bank, and with the weir height sloping down towards the low water outlet; so that a shingle bank, to be loved by seatrout, would form above the weir – where we could conveniently catch them of an evening. Fortunately I guessed that if a weir, *not* cobbled or cemented, is to withstand many floods, the biggest boulders must form its base and the front edge must not slope up steeply. We were lucky. Given the boulders available and the limitations of our only tool, I think, though I say it myself, we made as good a job of it as we could. To say that it was the best seatrout pool in the river for several years does not do it justice. But every silver cloud has its lead lining: so many seatrout stayed in the Long Pool that Gordon's up-stream was under-populated; and you had to queue in the evening to fish the Long Pool.

The new Long Pool was completed on schedule and we moved up-stream to the relatively minor task of repairing the Mill Pool weir. We would have finished there ahead of schedule but for a mini-flood. Next morning, I peered through the bushes which grew between the top twenty yards of the Long Pool and the path up above it. I was astonished to find it stiff with salmon and big seatrout. There was also a good sprinkling of both below the trees along the bottom twenty yards. Naturally the middle third was empty. The path was a popular walk for people who lived nearby, and a dog could not walk there, seven feet above the water, without making fish rush for shelter. If only I'd had a cast then. Conscientiously I proceeded to supervise completion of the Mill Pool. I thought the fish would wait until the afternoon.

They would have done if left in peace. But a very senior Club member had seen them too. Casting over them would have needed a little roll cast, side cast or steeple cast, or, preferably, wading to the other bank through the shallows twenty yards up-stream. He had made a snap decision: to remove all the bushes to permit a back cast without wading. When I got back, late that afternoon, the cutting had started. The few salmon left were circling uneasily near the tail. I pleaded with the man who was committing this sacrilege to desist until the committee could be consulted, but to no avail. The hatchet man had been told to do this job, but not that the committee had made me responsible for the whole operation. So what should have become the Club's best salmon pool, and its only easy salmon fly cast, remained empty of salmon, unless in coloured water.

Its productivity as a seatrout pool later tailed off, owing to less wanton sacrilege. Some walkers apparently enjoyed watching the fish, especially at the tail where the shoal of seatrout was thickest. They cut branches so that they did not have to bend their heads, and this gave the fish a good view of their watchers. The culminating event was simply an excess of zeal by the estate's foresters. Their alloted job was to brash the conifers on the *other* side of the path. For good measure they brashed all branches within reach off the sycamores which screened the lower third of the pool. Deprived of all privacy, no fish but a few finnock hung around in that pool any more. Incidentally, the Mill Pool, when it was back to its original depth, became our best salmon pool at all water levels. It was also popular with nocturnal netsmen despite my attempt to forestall this with some strategically placed boulders. Barbed wire plays hell with nets, but also with nylon lines, as we had to explain to one of our earlier keepers who had shown some initiative. The initial success of this venture spurred the Club to raise the money and save up for more improvements.

Cutting riverside trees and shrubs is not, of course, always disastrous, as it was on our new Long Pool. But in little rivers it should never be done lightly, for their anglers should treasure foliage which screens passing humans from the fish, or provides shade from the sun, and caterpillars, etc., for trout and seatrout. At dusk the latter species will leave their cover to feed in, and be caught in, streamy water or gravel beds. On big rivers, however, failure to cut self-seeded trees is often culpable negligence. On Upper Dess two neglected pools are fully fishable again, thanks to Harry's cutting. On Stobhall, Stankend, from the left bank, is a splendid taking place with a spinner in big floods. Unfortunately, one can then fish only the top half, and cannot follow a hooked fish down-stream. In the lower part, trees with boughs awash would catch your spinner and will snag some of the fish you hook.

About making weirs to create new pools, our stretch of the Ogwen was as tough a nut as could be found. The snags were its steep gradient – a drop of about 200 feet in two river-miles, and also the fact that a deluge in the mountains came straight off those rocks into the upper river and its feeder lakes. During a big flood you could hear the boulders bumping down the river bed before being in sight of the water. Traces remain of former *cobbled* weirs in places where the gradient was too steep. Even so, our Club's money was not all wasted.

Later, under new management, we made two more attempts. In the first, the River Board officials had to be persuaded not to try to repeat their success on the Seiont by building a chain of successive pools. The gradient of the stretch of the Ogwen which they fancied for this purpose was much steeper than on that mile of the Seiont. Except at the top, where nature had done half the work already. There, in hitherto wasted water, we made a pool, which after seven seasons was still a holding pool for salmon and seatrout. Despite my misgivings, we let them make one pool just below it. As feared, much of that weir was soon washed away. It remained, however, quite a good high water cast, though not, as it was at first, a holding pool. That operator of the excavator had by now become an expert. One could explain in a few minutes just what was wanted, then leave the rest to him.

Unfortunately his health obliged him to give up this type of work and my last such task proved much the most difficult. The so-called 'Keeper's Pool' was then just a pocket for salmon, conserved as such by two huge boulders. My plan was to make it a sizeable pool, about sixty yards long in high water. It required a strong and relatively long weir. The new operator was new at this game. Some of the work had to be redone, and in the end the job was rushed before our machine hours ran out. My specifications were not fully carried out, and part of that weir departed next winter. Still, most of it remained and after four seasons it held more salmon than before the operation, and seatrout too.

Thus, even in that difficult stretch of river, the cost and effort was, I think, well worthwhile. All such improvements are, of course, temporary. In any river nothing is permanent. In the flat mile of the Ogwen in Penrhyn Park, there is a cobbled weir still intact, *but* above it only gravelled up shallows. Since, however, our pool-making improved our catches even in the most awkward parts of the Ogwen, such operations could pay handsome dividends in many more suitable rivers. I offer to some young Scotsman on the make a golden opportunity – the formation of Mac . . .'s Fishing Pool Construction Company.

Fishing in mixed company
Through a friend I had booked a rod on an unfamiliar beat. I took the risk of making a 'blind date' with those who would take the other two rods. When I met the first of them in the hotel on Sunday evening, I got a shock. Had he been acting the role of the snob, all critics would have protested about his over-playing the part. I had to listen to bombinations about the lower orders, wogs – and Scots. Having failed to change the subject, or to get in edgeways that he was talking to a Scot, my heart sank at the thought of fishing with him all week. Would I be able to refrain from venting opinions or starting arguments which would cause disharmony? It was such a relief when the third angler appeared in the bar – his wife. No-one could have been less of a snob. She established immediate *rapport* with everyone she met. Whenever her spouse embarked on his favourite topic she cut him short and talked about fishing. His other conversational topic, ventilated when she was not present to dam the flow, was the things which he owned – companies, grouse moors, salmon river, etc.

What puzzled me was that he should be sharing with me an inexpensive beat, and staying in the same friendly but unpretentious hotel. On the first afternoon the jolly ghillie confided to me that the lady had confided to him that her husband was no good at fishing. 'As if I needed to be told', he added. The ghillie had been quick to size up the situation. He had to distribute three anglers between two very long pools. He checked that I was capable (just) of the difficult wading in the necks of each stream. He recognised that the lady was not an experienced angler, but very keen and learning fast. The other angler had to be parked on flat grass close to the bottles kept in his car. The ghillie popped back occasionally to replace missing flies on the gentleman's cast and to have a quick drink. He spent the rest of the day trying to ensure that the lady caught a salmon. Three of us displayed delight when she succeeded in this.

I too had sized up the situation on Monday. In a falling freshet, the salmon were going through this stretch like express trains. I had a chance in the top of one pool, but very little in the other, which required a left-handed roll cast longer than I could manage. Still, it was obvious that the longest pool must be one of the best seatrout pools in the river. I did not overtire myself that day, for a warm midgy evening was coming. I did not hear the end of the snob's postprandial oration in the bar. (His wife was letter-writing). I left for the river.

It was better than I could have hoped – about 150 yards of easy wading, with seatrout showing all the way down. Not that I got anything like all the way down. I must have started near the head of the shoal, among the big ones, too big to net. So it took some time playing each and returning to the bank to beach them. I then made the first mistake which led to my undoing. Sometimes a third hand would be a help and I used my mouth instead. This time, holding the rod in the right, I hurled a dead seatrout with the left towards the higher grass, *with the double-hooked tail fly in my mouth*. The fish hit my line fair and square and I was hooked up to the hilt in my lower lip, fortunately not in both lips or I could not have had another cigarette. It did not hurt much, so I went on fishing for half an hour. Perhaps it was the nicotine. The lip stung and was swelling. I decided that since I had five more nights ahead, it would be sensible to get someone in the hotel to cut out the hook, if anyone was still awake and sober.

The proprietor was both, but he insisted on 'phoning and awakening the nearest doctor. If I had known how far from near he lived I would have tackled the job myself. It took only two minutes when at last I found him. My second mistake was to mention to the lady next morning that I had caught a few seatrout: and she went and inspected them in the kitchen. I don't think she had seen one before. She decided to catch one. She was strong-willed.

The result was hard on her husband, and on me, and, I think, on the ghillie who had to work overtime for the first halves of the ensuing nights. The only place where he could station the husband was again on the short piece of flat grass close to his car. Unfortunately this was in the middle of *the* seatrout pool. He stood there swaying for an hour or so – safe, since the water was much too shallow to drown in. His sporting wife was free to fish all the way down from there. She did wade a bit with thigh boots, but not far enough. I had to spend my evenings as well as my days negotiating the most awkward boulders I have ever waded among; knowing that my chance of catching seatrout in that very fast water was minimal. One evening I had the consolation of two lovely salmon on a seatrout fly around midnight.

I would not have minded if the lady had caught a seatrout. I wanted her to succeed. Like the ghillie, I gave her advice and flies. She rejoined her husband, who had long been waiting in the car, at 2 or 3 a.m. When they had gone, I had a quick cast in *the* pool, but the seatrout had then lost their appetites. On entering the hotel after 3 a.m. one morning, I heard a stream of unprintable language issuing from the bar. Perhaps he had had an audience when he started and had not noticed its departure. He did notice me when I peered in to see if a brawl was in progress. He started again from the beginning. The gist of it was this: that he had that evening played a large salmon right to the bank, but that so and so ghillie had lost it for him – instead of gaffing the fish, he had grabbed the rod and pulled the fly from the fish's mouth. The ghillie shook with laughter when he gave me his account next day – the gentleman's fly had stuck on a stone, and for fifteen minutes he and his bending rod had remained stationary; so the ghillie had taken the rod, made a false cast with a lengthened line and released the fly. He was, however, pleased that the gentleman had obtained, if nothing else, a good fishing story.

I regret that my own story has no climax. Only an anticlimax. I had decided that on Saturday evening I would say to the lady something like: 'Fair's fair. I'm paying a third of the rent. Please may I complete my third of the seatrout fishing and have, or at least share with you, *the* pool tonight.' Unfortunately my friend who had arranged the lease had forgotten to tell me that this was to be a five-day week. As I learned *on Saturday morning*, the proprietor was to fish that day, and did. On saying goodbye to the lady, I learned that she intended to persuade her spouse to return for the same week next season. It was clear that her husband, poor chap, was destined to play the demanding role familiar to many a wife wed to a fishing addict.

I could say 'Thon was no my week.' The jolly ghillie undertook to get my salmon smoked and forwarded to me. He did in the end, about Christmas time, post the fish, which had apparently been kept in a well heated cottage. Fortunately my Springer spaniel was very fond of the odour of smoked salmon, and not at all fussy about flavour, colour or texture. He had a lovely time – smoked salmon for weeks; and he wasn't sick. Unfortunately this gave him such a taste for salmon that he continued to eat them, unsmoked and uncooked, when they were lying on the bank. To give him credit, he does start with the tail and fins and, with luck, I remember before he gets much further. It can, however, be embarrassing when it is someone else's spring fish, and they are selling at £2 or £3 per pound *unchewed*.

4
Variety in Methods

I may have given the impression that I am a fly snob. This is not so. Admittedly I started as a 'fly only' angler, and this form of angling still gives me most pleasure by far. It is also the most productive method in suitable conditions. Let us, however, start with a section on:

***Laissez-faire* and its limits**
A few game fishers may fish for the pot, but nearly all of them fish for fun. It is not for some of them to legislate about what does, or should, provide most fun for the others. Trout fishers now run into millions. I am glad that the pleasures of angling are so widely shared and that technology has enabled 'still waters' to be much more fully exploited. I am out of touch with some of the methods now used in such waters, and with flies like the Muddler, but what's in a name? Apparently it takes big fish. I do feel *some* qualms about the Cork Tip fly. (Presumably you can smoke the cigarette, before using the butt as a fly?) I have no doubt that this is the best imitation of the pellets on which the trout have been farm-fed and that it will 'take' them very quickly after they have been 'put', i.e. released from the stew pond. (The system is called 'Put and Take'.) I am not being snobbish. Each to his taste. I prefer wild trout, even though I have often failed to tempt them. I am not, however, in a position to throw stones, even at the Cork Tip fly.

I shall make a confession. During that post-war bonanza, Jim and I discovered a lovely loch hidden from the road by pine trees. We caught a few good brownies and rainbows in the morning. At sandwich time, a crust was absent-mindedly thrown on the water. Before you could say 'Izaac Walton', it had disappeared. I could now recognise a 'head and tail' rise, and that really was one. I forget which of us started the experiment, with a *small* crust on the tail fly, for we were

Fish in custody. Above: A Dee springer with fish-eating Springer.

Below: A Conway seatrout c/o trustworthy cat.

Two bonny seatrout. *Arthur Oglesby*

Beaching a fish—the author's preferred method. *Grace Oglesby*

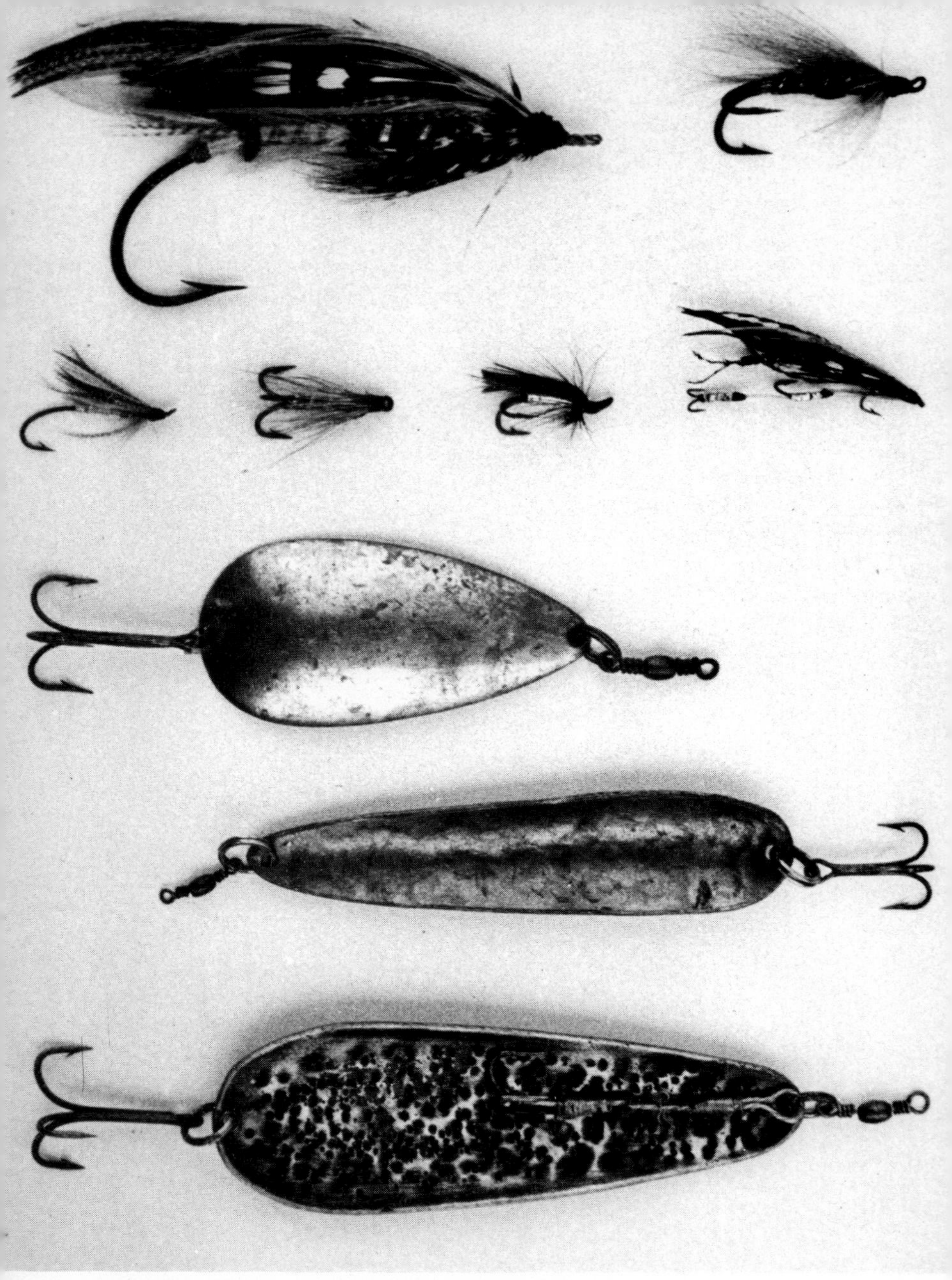

Flies and spoons favoured by the author. From left (top to bottom) Antique Jock Scott; Hairy Mary No. 2; Logie 8; Drury's Hairy Mary 8; Butcher 10; Sea Trout lure. Old-fashioned 2½in. spoon; Blair spoons—slim and fat.

nearly out of bread. It was our biggest success ever in the art of dry fly fishing. So easy. We did not need floatants. The crusts had no time to get waterlogged. The big rainbows had been well trained. We were lunching on the bit of grass, nearest to the road and favoured by picnickers. It was quite exciting. The rainbows saw the crusts from afar, and came at them like sword-fish, twisting, as they took the fly, in a tight U-turn. When the bread ran out, we had all we wanted. Oddly enough, having added this crumb to our know-how, we did not use it again. I do not think its owner would wish me to divulge the name of that loch. I suspect that the rainbows had been 'put'.

Nor am I in a position to throw stones at practitioners of another 'still water' technique. They have developed a method which I happened to discover when awaiting my examination results at St. Andrews. (I have recently learned that others had used this technique much earlier. See Conrad Voss Bark's accounts of his grandfather's exploits at Blagdon.) Cameron reservoir held some big trout. Occasionally one caught them on a big sedge-type fly at dusk. One afternoon when there was no wind, I experimented idly from the dam wall with a seatrout demon on the tail, letting it sink. However long I waited, it never reached the bottom, but when my patience ran out I pulled in the line with small jerks. This put sedge flies in the shade where they belong.

I passed on this secret to a lecturer, who later fished for Scotland. He did not keep the secret. He found that it also worked from boats. (Hence his Scottish Cap?) With this rather monotonous technique, the further you can cast your minnow-imitating 'fly', the better your chances. Hence the trays carried on the tummy on which to fold retrieved line. Hence, also, the danger that some innocent out of date trout fisher may pay for a trout rod, only to discover that he has been sold one which needs salmon line to make it work properly. This once happened to me. The distinguished firm which did the deed declined to add an extension piece to the butt, so that I could use it as a double-handed salmon rod. It has hung unused for fifteen years.

Of course I do not scoff at methods which have given me fun, even if they do not do so any longer. One does, as Viscount Grey put it, 'become more fastidious as to the kind of sport'. For me, one effect of ageing has been, increasingly, that the fun comes from achieving what is least easy. (I do not, however, subscribe to the ethical theory of Kant – that moral virtue belongs only to the Will of a person who overcomes his unruly desires. I have a spontaneous and sometimes troublesome desire to try to win against the odds.) It is similar to what happens to mountaineers. At first, it is a sufficient achievement to get to the top and find your way home. Then you need thirty Munros (Scottish peaks of 3,000 feet or over) to qualify you for joining the Scottish Mountaineering Club. Then it is rock faces which provide the challenge, and you progress, if you survive, from the 'difficult' routes via the 'severe' towards the impossible. (The 'difficult' ones were usually much too difficult for me.) I have never met a mountaineer who sneered at the chaps who walk hills for the view, even if they stick to well-worn paths. Of course I do not scoff at brother anglers who tread paths which I once trod.

There are, of course, limits to *laissez-faire*. I do not think I can improve on John Stuart Mill's way of delineating the limit, namely: provided that your actions do not interfere with the opportunities of others to pursue their pleasures in their own ways. This paraphrase is rather free, but for the present purpose it will do. I am not, like Mill, concerned with providing a criterion for choosing good laws, but rather a test of good manners. No angler will find it hard to think of examples which fail this test. Like those chaps who carry searchlights when night fishing for seatrout, and then direct them all over the pool; first to get visual evidence of the identity of anglers on the opposite bank, then every time they wade in, and whenever they wade out, and throughout playing and landing fish, and sometimes, I suppose, just to test the batteries. I think that their searchlights must be strapped on. I have always been too dazzled to see. When it starts I look for another pool.

How anti-social can anglers get? I shall give an even more distressing example. The Long Shot, near the foot of the Benchil mile of the Tay, looks the loveliest fly water that anyone could imagine, all 200 yards of it. There seems to be no danger of their lines crossing even if fly fishers, making thirty-yard casts, were wading from opposite banks. Having seen it in April, I had been counting the days until the 20 July. The privilege of fishing that pool for the rest of July would, I thought, repay the cost of the ticket for the other ten weeks when I could not use it. When I arrived, however, there were nine or ten competitors on each side, all hurling big purple prawns on enormous orange floats, which looked like speed-boats when swinging round and then being wound in. There was no down-the-pool, step-between-each-cast system. If they had tried that on the far bank, they would all have bumped into the river bailiff, who had chosen the bottom stand so that the running fish would see his prawn first.

Some of the ticket members turned out to be anglers who carried, and sometimes waved, fly rods; and others who had joined the prawn fishers said that they too would much prefer to be fishing with fly. I took it upon myself to convey the request that a *little* of the best fly water should be banned for the prawn. The answer that I got was this: the owner of one bank did not care *how* fish were caught, but did care about *how many*, which determines the market value of the fishery, and the use of prawns had bumped up the catches no end. There was no point in arguing against such reasoning.

Trout methods

This section will be brief. I have nothing new or unorthodox to contribute. The literature of angling provides many classics devoted to this subject, in which, progressively, art has been combined with science. During the twentieth century this applies especially to expertise in use of the dry fly and more recently the nymph. I fear that my only contribution can be to encourage those who lack time or even inclination to make their trout fishing a branch of applied science – by reassuring them that the fun of catching trout can still be obtained by simple and old-fashioned methods of fly fishing. This is true, at least for those who fish in Scottish rivers or lochs.

I do not regard it as a virtue to have remained old-fashioned in my methods. I regret being still so unsophisticated. This is partly a result of my getting seduced by salmon and seatrout. My experience of trout fishing has been almost entirely confined to using flies, and mostly wet flies. Until I met the Parachute fly, my occasional would-be dry fly was also usually wet. I am, however, extremely ignorant about entomology. I can recognise the kinds of flies which look most like Greenwell's Glories, March Browns and a few others. I have not yet identified the insects which most of the patterns in my collection are (presumably) meant to imitate. I do not even know whether I have seen a real live May-fly. If I have, it did not look like the imitations which have been waiting in my fly boxes for their turn for nearly forty years.

My entomological ignorance has not, however, prevented me from enjoying the classics written about the chalk streams. I find spell-binding their lyricism about fly life (and weeds) and the names of their upright imitations. But the trout in the Scottish and Irish waters which I have fished are certainly less fastidious than those of the Test and the Itchen. In Scottish rivers the trout have usually seemed content with small thinly-dressed spiders, as recommended by Stewart. Presumably these are mistaken for nymphs. I have not found that it makes very much difference whether the hackle came from a badger, a partridge, a snipe or a water-hen. When fishing the lochs in the North West, I have found nothing to beat rather large

Zulus, Palmers and Worm flies – more wingless wonders – but I have no idea for what these are mistaken by the trout. In the lochs in the lowlands of Scotland, small winged flies are what I have found most effective. Those in which I would there have most faith, at any rate when some fish are breaking the surface, are as follows. On the tail a Peter Ross (apparently representing a shrimp), on the bob position a Greenwell or a Butcher, and in the middle a Blae and Black or a Woodcock Mixed (with red and yellow body). It usually pays, however, to use at least one of the local favourites. For example, Rogan's Rough Olive proved to be the trouts' favourite on the Drowes and Lough Melvyn.

To trout specialists this advice about flies may appear simplistic. I had better add that quite often the patterns you choose seem less important than how you use them. Until one has found what is currently enticing to the trout, it pays to keep varying the speed and style of movement of the flies, and their depth. For spells when no surface-feeding trout are visible, one should have ready to hand a cast adapted for fishing deep. Nowadays I would use one with leaded nymph and shrimp fly. Before such flies were available, I used small double hooks to make the flies sink faster. For fishing deep, my team of flies included at least one 'attractor', like a Dunkeld or Alexandra (imitating baby fish?) and at least one spider or Palmer (deputising for nymphs?).

When the trout remain dour and one cannot resist the urge to keep trying another pattern, the tail fly is most convenient for such experiments. It is easier to add a foot of nylon to the end of a shortened cast than to retie droppers. I think it important, at any rate with winged flies, that they hang and swim the right way up. No doubt experts at tying knots achieve this at the first attempt. But despite a lot of practice, I may need two or three attempts before the angle of a dropper fly meets my approval, so the length of the dropper may have grown too short before I succeed.

My earlier fishing with wet flies on lochs was sometimes too easy, especially on Lintrathen reservoir, then under-fished with only three boats. One morning there, Jim and I inadvertently caught the limit of thirty-six trout by noon. If the boatman had told us the score at thirty-five, we could have fished for six more hours for one for the taxidermist. The cunning man wanted an afternoon free for gardening. When the Ballathie trout converted me to the more exacting art of dry fly fishing, this did not leave much time for further progress. (Otherwise I might have qualified as a dry fly man.) However, a year and a half later I departed to Wales. Regarding trout fishing in

Snowdonia, my hopes were raised by the books of Frank Ward and W. M. Callichan. These hopes were disappointed. One would expect that in those acid mountain lakes, however small the trout, they would at least be hungry. Apart from my first visit to Llyn Conwy, when half-pounders took a Blae and Black quite frequently, the many lakes that I tried proved most ungenerous. The fish would spurn even my Coch-y-Bonddu. Perhaps they required one to sing to them in Welsh. I had to readjust myself to averaging one keepable trout per outing, and such outings became much less frequent. More recently 'put and take' reached North Wales, but I was not tempted. For I found that the taking, with maggots, worms and spinners, started very early when, even in sub-tropical Wales, fly life was still in abeyance.

Seatrout methods

I shall say rather more on this topic, since I have done a little experimenting; and also because the seatrout has been unduly neglected in angling literature. There are very few books devoted to seatrout fishing, notably those by R. C. Bridgett, Jeffery Bluett, Hamish Stuart and Falkus. I find this surprising since I regard the seatrout as the most game and certainly the most dashing of the salmonidae.

My first seatrout was caught with the help(?) of a maggot on the fly, but I never became enamoured with maggots. An Edzell angler had left me to dangle my flies plus maggots from a rocky ledge far above a deep pool. He then disappeared into the dark and I never saw him again. I groped my way back to our holiday home with a pounder which I had had to lift up several feet from the North Esk to the rock. Later, my occasional experiments with maggots did not enamour Sheila. She did not like my keeping them in the fridge, despite the fact that this prolongs their active life and they could not escape from the tin. I have reached the conclusion that their presence on a fly is superfluous. In my night fishing experiments, I used one (or two) maggots only on the dropper of a two-fly cast. (They survive longer there than on the tail fly.) Yet nearly all my fish were taken on the tail fly.

In my earlier sessions of dusk and night fishing, when I used single hooks, I found it frustrating to have so many snatches or pulls from fish which did not stay hooked. The next stage was to use double hooks, which are much more efficient. The final stage was to start with doubles, and to change, when it was really dark, to a demon armed with one or two little single hooks plus a tiny double at the rear end. I had these tied in sizes ranging from three-quarters to two inches. It was very unusual to lose a fish which mouthed them, and they got a generous share of the bigger fish. Some nights, of course, never get dark enough for demons, or for other big flies, depending on the moon.

In Scottish rivers, where seatrout are not so shy as Welsh sewin and are catchable in full daylight, fly pattern may be important. Certainly on the Spey a gold-bodied fly 'Stuart's Fancy' did better than any other, for me at least. In the Dee, where summer salmon like diminutive flies, a No. 10 or 12 Stoat's Tail seems to be equally welcome to seatrout, provided that your cast is of rather light nylon. But when the light has departed, whether it is seatrout or sewin that you are after, you need something bigger, say a No. 6 or a demon on the tail. As for pattern, it does not seem to matter, so long as it has a really opaque wing, which looks black against an almost black sky, and as long as the body is silver to reflect any glint of light that is going; in other words, I recommend a Butcher or an Alexandra. Throughout some seasons I have fished only with Alexandras. I would be equally confident with Butchers. These, of course, are cheaper, as ducks are more plentiful than peacocks. Stupidly, I have wasted money by ordering Alexandra-style, peacock-herl, demons – prettier to human eyes.

The Conway, however, was different. I refer to the period when at least two of its pools got choked with huge seatrout. Having seen a few from Harry's fridge and heard some of his tales about Hafod, I took a rod on 'Mrs. Green's stretch', because it included the second most populous pool for these monsters – the Wall Pool. When, later, I read Falkus's book *Seatrout Fishing*, I found that much of what Falkus had learned for himself, Harry had independently discovered. He taught me his 'secrets'. The big ones, weighing up to twenty pounds, were catchable on fly only in the blackest part of moonless nights. He attached great importance to the length of the sinking tip whipped to the floating line. The fly which he used for the big ones was a light 'streamer' fly, about 1½ in. long, silver-bodied and hair-winged.

I savoured only a very small sample of Harry's excitements. As often as not I arrived at the Wall Pool to find mist rising from the water. When conditions seemed to be right, the stream of traffic whose headlights shone on the water seemed to go on all night. My most exciting evening was when a shoal of the monsters had just come off the tide and were slapping around exploring the pool, but alas they were not yet settled enough to take. In two seasons I got only one 'Bottle fish' (over 11 lb). It fought like a flounder and tasted like a kelt. Still the Dry Fly Sherry was palatable and the fish looked handsome in a photograph. I had to share this pool with so many others that I decided to settle for the Ogwen, whereby I saved an hour's driving and could rely on much more continuous rod bending. I pass on the information, however, for those still young enough to dispense with sleep. Note that night fishers need extra food. Sheila still tells people about the occasion when, in the small hours, I ate all of the rhubarb and custard, and only learnt later, by chance, that the custard had been fish sauce. I did at the time get a vague impression of an interesting taste sensation, but then I would have swallowed anything.

What I have said about the unimportance of fly patterns, needs one more qualification. For ease of reference, I shall christen the fly in question 'Forster's Favourite' (FF), after the friend who gave me a few in case I should ever want seatrout from salt water. Later I found that I did. Exploring the Outer Isles, Sheila and I happily found Rodel in Harris. The hotel was most relaxed and informal. If it had a clock, it was apparently kept as an ornament. Fishing times determined meal times, not vice versa. They seemed to have about ten seatrout lochs per bedroom. Unfortunately they also had a drought, and the seatrout were still in salt water savouring trickles of fresh water at high tides. Fortunately boats were available to meet this crisis, and boatmen. FF was my honoured tail fly, and it distinguished itself. The other hotel anglers had given up, but seatrout came back on the menu. Sheila did not miss my company. Accompanied by a spirited Cambridge don she searched for and sighted a pair of golden eagles. In case others should need it, FF is very simple: a low-slung white wing, white hackle, silver body, no tail. It must represent some tiny, tasty, fish.

I feel that a seatrout deserves a better fate than a worm hook down its gullet. I never mastered the art of flood fishing in dirty water with the worm below the tip of a fly rod, swum under the bank. I have watched experts do it often enough. Evidently one needs to know each corner of the under-water bank, and to keep adjusting the amount of lead, so that the worm swims in mid-water – or a little lower if you want to prevent it passing too high over a passing salmon's head. My own impatient method when I play the worm game is to tape a spinning reel on a fly rod, chuck the bait up-stream, wind enough in to avoid slack line, and then have a little walk. Once at least it worked like a charm on an Ogwen pool. (I had just designed it and supervised its construction.) There was an unexpected flood early in June, and I had two free hours before the next batch of examination papers would await me. I had seen *one* sea-trout in that pool the day before. Being a dilettante with the worm, my only hooks were tatty, tiny, two-hook Pennell tackles. I got four fat seatrout totalling sixteen pounds. Had my hooks been bigger or sharper, or the tying less frayed, I should have had ten. Never before nor since did I witness such a run there so early. Never have I known seatrout make fiercer fights for freedom. I did not grudge the ones that got away. At least they were only lip-hooked. When using tiny Pennells you can strike at a touch. I prefer this to waiting for single worm hooks to be swallowed.

There are several methods of catching seatrout with which my acquaintance is nil or negligible, like Quill Minnows and Dapping. I fancy Dapping, however, especially having to recite a prayer, for example, before you strike. I have been ready to start reciting throughout the day on a few of the finest seatrout lochs of the North West. To *my* eyes, my huge Loch Ordie fly kept tripping the waves irresistibly. All that I got were finnock which had hooked themselves before I knew what had happened. What baffled me was how so unerringly they got so much fly into so little mouth. On one last day, I decided to find if there was anything bigger in the loch. My wet flies produced a nice basket of two pounders, and some expressions of respect at last from a hitherto tongue-tied boatman.

I mentioned earlier the Minister who assured me that in Scotland trout fishing is free. When I first met him, I was about to start fishing a hill loch. He was setting off in the (absentee landlord's) boat, since it was easier for him to row three miles than to walk, *en route* for a more remote and better trout loch. I was young, and brown trout were the limit of my horizon. My casts were of light and well-worn *gut*. I cannot go back now; now that I know that this loch, in July, is full of large seatrout and salmon. I wish I could. I ran out of casts. Each of the supposed trout which took my sunk fly, allowed me to feel a little of its weight, but only momentarily. I think that they must have been very big seatrout. Surely salmon would not be so crazy for No. 10 Zulus and Palmers? I have now lost that irrational faith that the more remote the loch, the better the fishing. My bias is now for lochs accessible from the sea, where seatrout fishing sometimes also yields big brownies or even a salmon as a pleasant surprise.

Salmon methods

Having acknowledged my preference for the fly, I shall start with other methods. I do not scorn them like Andrew Lang who wrote: 'A bait-fisher *may* be a good man, as Izaac was, but it is easier for a camel to pass through the eye of a needle.' The prawn is not my *bête noire*, however dyed, *if* it is fished with discrimination; as it was by that free fisher of the Tay who left his deputy to manage the Bank so often in July. His policy was to pick one first-class pool, and keep fishing it all day. On the Tay, fishing a pool normally takes an hour or more. He sometimes risked a warning from Mr. MacRae, and *once* in the day, would show a prawn to the fish all the way down the pool, but taking less time than usual. He would then rush back and fish it, more carefully, with a fly. He did catch an odd fish on the prawn; and he sometimes gave a running commentary on the fish that were nosing, lipping, or admiring, his prawn. He certainly got a lot of these curious (excited?) fish on the flies which duly followed the prawns.

That is one kind of discriminating prawn fishing. I have not followed his example. I got intimidated by the authors who affirm that the mere sight of a prawn is liable to empty of salmon your bit of the river. When I have a week to fish a beat, I keep a few prawns (or shrimps) in case we are desperate on Saturday afternoon. I never use them unless I am showing them to fish which I know are there. Then if they are *on* the prawn, one gets one in the first two or three casts. In that case I carry on until they are *off* it. If I do not get a fish, or have the whiskers bitten off, my prawn fishing is finished within five or ten minutes. It *is* sport. It is not only in the Spey that prawn-hooked fish move with extra velocity. I may ask Harry to write an Appendix on shrimp fishing. Should he break a leg, he might find time, but perhaps not the inclination since he now eschews bait fishing.

The only rivers on which I have caught salmon with worms are rather far apart – the Slaney, the Ogwen and the Morar. Some worm fishers are quite successful in the Tay, but there I suspect that they start with a close inspection of the river bed as (or by) skin-divers. I lose patience after losing six or seven carefully baited hooks. This takes me only about twenty minutes, fifteen of them replacing hooks, lead wire and worms. But after Fitz's lesson, I sometimes tried it on the Ogwen, on the day after a flood, or even the next day. It was very successful, though not prolonged, as Sheila's compost heap did not produce many worms.

My technique was rather similar to up-stream spinning. I used the same reel. From well below the lie, I hurled the bunch of worms to land about ten yards above it, with enough lead wire to make them trundle down the gravel past the fish. To keep loose contact, I wound in, with rod high, ready to drop the rod and free the line when a fish took hold, to take worms back to its lie. The best pool for this being the one below Half-Way Bridge, I sometimes had spectators, fortunately not close enough to cross-examine me.

Spinning next – and I have let slip, in passing, some of my views about this. Everyone knows that in early spring one's lure should pass, slow and deep, over the salmon's noses. Not everyone seems to know the converse. Throughout the summer, the Tay harlers' favourite lure is 'the Louis', officially named 'the Kynoch Killer'. (I don't suppose that they ever spell their nickname. I am assuming that it is named after the kings of France.) It is the biggest plug known to man. Even when harling in low water, they often use one on each rod. I am prejudiced. I am a Jonah in the boat. I do, however, keep two Loo-ies (my own plural), in case I have a guest who wants a rest. I also keep a strip of sorbo rubber for a guest's posterior. Boat seats grow harder as you wait for a rod to bend.

The converse, of course, is that when the water has warmed up, fresh-run fish will make a dash for something small and moving fast. It is not only on the Ogwen that up-stream casting and fast winding pays dividends. One of Hardy Brothers discovered this, I think on the Coquet, several decades ago. They introduced their little heavy-weight, blue and silver devons precisely for this purpose. They explained the technique in a catalogue which I have lost. The other brothers who won that competition in 1956 for Cargill and Stobhall had evidently read that catalogue. When the grilse were running, the piles of them on their banks grew quite high. In small rivers like the Ogwen, a Hardy heavy-weight would be boulder-fast before you started winding. The problem there is to find $1\frac{1}{4}$ or $1\frac{1}{2}$ in. metal devons light enough to prevent this; and to throw them far enough, you have to use a lighter line than is desirable, except from the salmons' viewpoint.

I could air my prejudices about shapes, sizes and colours of spinning lures, but when in the mood for spinners, salmon are not very fussy. Mrs. Robertson told me of a Slaney angler who ran out of golden preserved sprats, made do with his yellow tooth-brush on his spinning mount – and went on catching fish. (He put the bristles at the front end, if you wish to try it.) So let us just stick each to his own prejudices about spinning lures. Instead I shall seize a different opportunity. Criticisms of tackle may not appear in fishing journals and thereby offend advertisers. I shall try to get into print, at last, a few moans. The foremost concerns those infuriating mounts for devons which are made of soft wire. When bent they stay bent, and they get bent at right angles every time the devon hits the water. Some firm has been mass-producing these for decades, and still is. Why should I have to throw them away (and where is it safe to throw them?) and then have to make replacements with Alasticum wire?

Why do tackle shops go on importing hooks (the French seem to be the worst) which bend straight under modest pressure? It is not so easy neatly to attach a new triangle to a certain imported spoon. Admittedly you do not lose them on the bottom – back they come with one, or even two, hooks almost straightened out. This is little consolation for the salmon which they lose for you. And why should I have to pay for some artist in the artificial minnow factory for painting white eyes on the lures? The effect, in the water, is to give them a white collar – but in the wrong place, well above the gills.

I mentioned earlier that I still prefer the spoon-shaped kind of spoons despite the Scandinavian works of art which flood the market. I admit that it is easier to throw a Toby spoon further, and in the intended direction. But my advice to use a fat spoon when you would otherwise be stuck with worming is worth a lot of fish. For once I shall offer a rule, if only a rough one which does not require a thermometer: if in normal light you can just see light-coloured stones when knee-deep, use a 2½ in. copper and silver spoon; if you can see such stones when up to your groin, use a 2 in. spoon. If you can see them when up to your chest, a devon will do. And seatrout, too, like spoon-shaped spoons.

One sometimes needs an otter to retrieve spinning lures. When fishing in summer in familiar rivers there is no excuse for getting your spinner stuck on the river bed. But unless you sometimes do this in the spring, you are not fishing properly. It is then that thrifty anglers need an otter. There are many varieties. I have seen an empty whisky bottle used for this purpose – an excuse, I think, for emptying it. It is not recommended, being too heavy and not of the right shape. Harry lent me a new design – a conveniently small disc made of wood. This saved the same Blair spoon a dozen times in a week. I wish that I had forgotten to return it. Instead I bought a pair of plastic otters of the same shape. Neither re-emerged from its first swim. A very efficient otter is easy to make, from a straight piece of wood about 10 or 12 in. long and 1½ in. diameter. A cord is tied to each end leaving nearly 20 in. dangling. A link, to slip on to your casting line, is attached to the cord a little off-centre. An optional extra is a little lead (the metal) on the lower end of the wood. This enables you to 'gie a good tug' coming from the direction of an angler located below you on the opposite bank. The most exciting use for such otters is to release a salmon which has tethered your line round a boulder by running up the far side of it. Once released, the fish, to put it mildly, acquires a new lease of life. Indeed the effect is nearly as dramatic as that of those bats on my bob fly.

I hope that is enough spinning lore. Writing about fly fishing will, for me, be more exacting – there is so much more from which to select – but also more exciting. I love even the flies themselves, and indeed their names. I am like Mill's miser: though a bank balance is really only of value as a means to other ends, the miser comes to love accumulating cash for its own sake. Now that I know I need only one pattern, I have acquired hundreds: to gloat over. The best bargain that I ever got (for £1) was 200 genuine antiques, left-overs from the collection of a peer whose descendants cared not for fishing. They tell one quite a lot about him – that he fished many rivers, that he had an eye for a good figure dressed in bold colours, and that, like me, he could not leave a tackle shop without acquiring his latest fancy.

These antiques had spent a century in a dark cupboard and are still in pristine condition, and scarcely any of the roped-gut eyes have been touched. I was touched that Great-Gran was so touched by her eighty-fifth birthday present, ready just in time. It was one of the Baron's biggest and most colourful specimens, mounted in a spare picture frame. 'It must be very valuable', she said, awed. 'Still you'll get it back when I'm dead.' Those antiques can still catch fish if you do not use the gut eyes. I proved it with a little (1½ in.) number. I left on it only enough of the original hook to form an anchor and rigged it with a small triangle – as an extra tail. (Alasticum wire has many uses.)

I have, in passing, mentioned some earlier stages in my education – the transition from the No. 1 Wilkinsons to Wood's Low Water Singles, then to Low Water Doubles (and Hardy Short-Point Doubles), and then to Drury flies. I did flirt briefly with Waddington's 'Elverine Lures'. They did not fetch me even an offer, perhaps because they did not evoke my faith. To my eyes, their triangle hooks look much too conspicuous to be worn by baby eels. Now we anglers never stop learning. My latest discovery – one that my first fly-caught grilse and salmon each tried to teach me – is that salmon, like seatrout, *love* the Butcher. There is a gaudy dressing in books on salmon flies which is also named 'the Butcher'. I am, however, referring to that simple dressing familiar to every trout fisher; which can be made even simpler by omitting the red tail. Unfortunately it is not mass-produced in doubles bigger than size 10.

I am sorry, Colonel Drury, but on your hooks, Butchers would be prone to swim upside down. Judging from my results on the Tay in recent years, all that we need are Butchers. Not the 'Bloody' ones or the 'Kingfisher' ones, but the simple silver-bodied Butchers; to be tied in a range of sizes on (preferably Low Water) double hooks. A simple job for a beginner in fly tying. Admittedly I have not yet used, or seen, such a Butcher on a No. 1 hook, suitable for the gloaming. I shall try this too at the first opportunity.

About using salmon flies, I tie them on so that they swim in line with the cast; then I cast and 'mend' and *concentrate* – on the unseen fish. (Curiously, I have never hooked a fish when I have concentrated on lighting a cigarette after casting.) I have not found it necessary to follow Wood in 'mending' the line several times as the fly comes round. He claimed to do this without jerking the fly, but I can't. So I do all of my mending in one go, as the fly hits the water. If the resulting spray from my rod, when *it* hits the water, wets the boat fishers, we should not be so close. One should, of course, not acquire the habit of mending without considering the water which one is fishing. In summer fishing, especially, a bit of a belly on the line to hasten the speed of the fly may help in the quieter water; sometimes also an inshore mend to try to tempt that fish which follows the fly. If it takes the fly 'at the dangle', then, lip-nipped, it usually splashes on the surface and is gone forever. Especially when one is fishing in a gusty wind with double- or treble-hooked flies, one should check regularly that they are not swimming sideways or back to front. Nothing can be more maddening than to discover this effect of a wind-knot after fishing a stretch full of salmon.

Salmon rods, like all rods, should, ideally, be old friends, removable extensions of your arms. But never go fishing without having available two friends of each species, in case a heifer chews, or walks on, one of them. If you are so old-fashioned as to use a Greenheart fly rod, it may break while casting normally. Greenheart salmon rods, though sweet and slow in their action, die fairly young from wood fatigue. But for my arthritic right shoulder, I should not have needed to go on acquiring more salmon fly rods. A casting champion once told me that the 12½-ft Wye was the best rod that Hardy's ever made. Mine, with a Perfect reel, was perfect. It still is, though together they weigh two pounds. Formerly when I wanted a rest and the smaller flies would do, my 11 ft Houghton sufficed. Since my right shoulder now protests even at the weight of a pen, I have had to find something lighter even than the Houghton, never mind the Sharpe's, the Cordon Bleu, etc.

Thank goodness they discovered carbon fibre in time. It was a revelation, as well as a relief, to discover this summer what could be done with a 10-ft rod weighing only 3½ oz. I found that I could throw

No. 9 floating line over twenty-five yards. That would not, however, have been possible had not Dermot Wilson foreseen the advantage of providing a five inch-extension to the butt, to enable it to be used double-handed. The maker says that this rod works with trout lines as light as AFTM 4; so it appears that I am going to complete my days as a one-rod man, as I was until I reached thirty.

Now that I know about the Butcher, thermometers are going to cost me more than flies. I keep leaving the former in the water whose temperature I am taking. I go on replacing them because I consider them indispensable. Without one you will go on getting some fish with a sink-tip line whatever the weather. But judging by my experience, Wood was dead right about the importance of the relative temperatures of air and water. My advice is to carry a spare spool for your fly reel, and to use a sink-tip line when the water is the warmer, but always a floater when the air is appreciably the warmer. If you fish fast glides where a floater results in flies skating on the surface, sacrifice a yard or so of the tapered tip of (preferably someone else's) Kingfisher trout line, which is slightly heavier than water.

Some fishing books have devoted a chapter to the gaff, more, I think, than it deserves. My telescopic gaff has its place – on a nylon cord hanging from my neck, alongside the thermometer, thus forming an attractive pendant. Such a gaff is an effective priest. You only need one bang. Recently, I have found a use for another type of gaff – the kind which screws into a long, strong, bamboo pole. If you remove the gaff head and bind a loop of nylon rope on the end of the pole which does not have the brass screw, you have the lightest possible wading stick. If you carry a gaff (or net), it is imprudent to use it on another's fish, unless at his request. You feel such an ass if you bungle it. Jim once rushed into the Spey to net a stranger's huge sea-trout – and lost it for him. I once mis-gaffed the only salmon hooked (lightly) by a guest. Each victim took the loss in his stride. The would-be helpers suffered most. I decline offers to help me land a fish to avoid the risk of emotional injury to my benefactor.

I have not yet bought a deerstalker, but it is prudent to wear one or something equally tough when casting a fly in a gale. I have twice had to ask the Perth infirmary to cut out a fly from the back of my scalp. Fortunately Perth was on the way home. Polaroid spectacles, invaluable for fish-watching, are also useful to protect your *eyes* from the flies. The Sack also deserves a mention. Never forget it. The day that you do is the day that you need it to carry your catch. The modern nylon sack is very robust. If you wash it when the smell in the car gets too strong, it will last for many years.

My last word about respectable methods of catching salmon is: Beware of sweeping generalisations. In books written by a one-river or perhaps a three-river angler, there is a tendency to make such generalisations, sometimes formulated as precise rules. For example, according to Richard Waddington & A.H.E. Wood, *either* you fish for salmon with an enormous fly as near to the river bed as possible *or*, if the air is warmer than the water, with a little fly a few inches below the surface, *or* you waste your time. If these anglers had fished little spate rivers in North Wales or North-West Scotland, they would not have been so dogmatic.

In the Ogwen in flood, or the turbulent pools of the Kirkaig, you need a rather large fly worked vigorously near the surface, whatever your thermometer tells you. If I have learned anything from fishing in a variety of waters, it is that dogmatism about methods is misplaced, that 'Always' and 'Never' are never justified. No. I had better qualify that generalisation! I have tried and failed to disprove one statement, found, I think, in one of Balfour-Kinnear's books, that a salmon will *never* take a fly while the sky is suffused with sunset colours. But I should be surprised if nobody had falsified it; and the rule is distinctly vague – how much of the sky or clouds must be suffused to make it hopeless? I have hooked fish when *some* clouds still glowed orange.

Dubious and nefarious methods

Unless I had read somewhere that 'cross-lining' is an illegal (and therefore obviously deadly) method of fly fishing for trout, this technique would never have occurred to me. Not at that age, anyway, when Jim and I were both in short trousers. I think it was during the holiday at Edzell that we found a tiny neglected dam. It was covered with weeds except for a patch in the middle and also a clear strip running to within a few yards of one of the four rectilinear banks. A few trout dimpled the unweeded water. In those days Jim still did what I told him. A loch cast was duly connected to the line of each rod. We walked down opposite banks, flies up in the air, until I had reached the place where it might have been possible to bring a fish ashore. Judging by our experience, legislators need not have wasted time on *that* law. We did achieve an effect somewhat similar to dapping, but such was the tautness and weight of the fifty yards of suspended line that the few trout which managed to catch a fly shook themselves off before Jim or I could pull some line off our reels. I could not recommend this method even if it were legal.

The allegation that guddling is an *easy* way of getting a trout for the pan must be a myth originating from earlier ages, when trout were much more numerous and trusting than our ancestors. I could have caught bucketfuls on fly during the many hours which I have spent trying to verify that it is possible at all. Ultimately I got one too small to eat. Not recommended, unless you enjoy wearing wet clothes, getting scratched and being eaten by horse-flies.

Setting lines with a large number of wormed hooks is, unfortunately, a method that must have occurred to every angler. I nearly got corrupted when too young to know that it was illegal. A man who wanted to show the boy how to make a killing went to enormous trouble. (It was not one-handed Alec.) Worms were scarce in Dalwhinnie, yet he found enough to bait about fifty hooks on Friday evening when they were left in Loch Ericht. We never found how many got swallowed. He rowed the boat hard into the shingle where the line had been secured to a boulder – and cut the line. He was left, cursing, with three yards of it – and a young soul snatched from burning. I know it is still done. I hope that the law is up to date. The fine, or the weeks in prison, ought to increase according to the cubic power of the number of hooks on the line.

Having thus been snatched myself, I have not indulged in the other activity called 'snatching'. I am told there are even some parties who spend the whole of their week *on the royal Dee* using spinners carefully adapted for foul-hooking (I will not reveal how). Apparently they get big catches, and for every fish landed there must be six or seven with open wounds to be invaded by bacteria. I must, however, confess that on the rare occasions when I have got a foul-hooked fish ashore *I have not put it back*. Indeed I have not yet met any other angler who claims to have done so. I fear that this makes us lawbreakers too. If so, the Law is an Ass. Would the hardest Hanging Judge have sent Great-Gran to prison for keeping that twenty-pounder hooked in the tail? Or me, when ultimately I wore out a salmon hooked at night in the dorsal fin by the tiny hooks on my devon? (During the time it took, I could have had its weight in sea-trout.) I know that it is not easy for legislators to describe unambiguously in legal prose the difference between such accidents and what those blighters do on the Dee, and in most other rivers. It is, however, very easy for a bailiff to recognise the difference. He only has to watch them operate, inspect their *very* strong lines and especially the things they put on the end of them. Up with their fines.

Having mentioned some dubious methods, I shall close this section with a joke told by my father-in-law. It took him much longer to tell it because he laughed for so long before he reached the poacher's point. The poacher was defending himself in Court. The case against him was that he had been apprehended beside the river 'with all the necessary equipment.' His defence was brief: 'You ought to charge me with rape too; I've also got all the necessary equipment for that.'

A good point, and well taken. Presence on a river bank with rods, reels and flies does not prove a man to be a fly fisher. My endorsement of that poacher's logic does not, of course, imply approval of his intended methods. Consider how Andrew Lang chided those who destroy sport 'in the sacred name of Liberty.' In his Introduction to the Everyman edition of *The Compleat Angler*, he cited, and I suspect wrote, this parody of Burns:

'Scots wha fish wi' salmon roe,
Scots wha sniggle as ye go,
Will ye stand the Bailie? No!
  Let the limmer dee.

Now's the day and now's the time,
Poison a' the burns wi' lime,
Fishing fair's a dastard crime,
  We're for fishing *free*!'

As Lang added, 'Free Fishing' of such kinds would soon spell no fishing at all.

A method of testing different methods

The study of Economics left one mark upon me, a habit which might, I suppose, be called a fetish – keeping statistics. I commend this fetish to anyone who might write a fishing book. As demonstrated above, it enables one to report the pattern and size of the fly responsible for any particular triumph or bereavement. More importantly, it provides a means of checking generalisations based upon one's fallible memory.

I have recorded the details about each salmon I have caught. Not *every* detail, like scale counts, whether I was smoking when it took, etc., but all that seemed relevant. Since paper got so costly I have not recorded the air and water temperatures when *each* fish took. Not only does it amuse me to record such history, it is also possible to learn from it – provided that one also analyses the data. My initial impetus to analyse was my dismay at the end of the first two seasons when I had fished for salmon. I had to record the wretched fact that I had landed only sixty per cent of my offers when spinning and only forty per cent on fly. Being a thrifty Scot, I had to improve on that.

I shall explain my recording system. At the end of each season, I add up the totals, separately for each river and also for each method (fly, spinning and, if any, worm and prawn). For each method, I then subdivide. The formula is: 'Pulls' + 'HCO' (hook came out) + 'Breakages' (ugh!) + 'Landed' = 'Offers'. The percentage of Landed to Offers provides an Index of my Inefficiency, and the figures in the other columns may help to reduce this. I must admit that the class 'Pulls' does leave room for some borderline cases. I do not, of course, count cases where the fly line just starts to straighten, or 'plucks', which might be trout or seatrout. As 'pull' suggests, I have to feel the weight of the fish, if only for half a second. However, I do not use a stop-watch. I could not take the oath that I have never dismissed as a mere pluck what was properly a pull (with an eye on the season's Inefficiency Index).

My statistics have shown some progress. They *had* to in respect of spinning. I started under the bad influence of Wanless, using nylon of only eight or even six pounds breaking strain. Naturally the effect of this was appalling. In my first two seasons the ratio of Breakages to Landed was one out of four! For the next nine seasons it averaged one in seven. Since then it has averaged one in twelve. The moral is that 35 mm. nylon is invisible to salmon in the clearest water. In recent seasons we have been able to buy stronger nylon for an extra 50p or so per drum – 30 mm. nylon which has the (nominal) breaking strain of 13 lb, the same as that of the standard 35 mm. stuff, and the stronger 35 mm. line has a (nominal) breaking strain of 18 lb. Now 50p is not much compared with the value of a salmon. Incredibly the good news does not seem to have reached many Tay salmon fishers, judging by my recent attempt to buy the stronger nylon in Perth. I found one spool in the third shop. False economy!

I have no idea how my spinning ratio, about seventy-five per cent of offers landed, compares with that of the average angler, though I am sure it is worse than Harry's. I did, however, have one really good period, when up-stream spinning on the Ogwen, during the last four years of that river's prime – forty-two salmon landed out of forty-eight offers. I attribute this to fishing only known lies and always being at the ready. This, in the case of spinning, means being ready to strike with the fingers *firm* on the reel handle. With the up-stream style, one still needs to strike when a fish grabs as it turns. I regard these figures as a freak. During my first season on the Ogwen, my spinning produced seven fish from seventeen offers. And the policeman who seemed to be free to fish every flood, claimed seven from thirty-five fish *hooked*. (He did not count mere pulls). Had I been less conscientious, I could have recorded forty-two out of forty-four. For four of the six events classified as pulls came in rapid succession – a school of visibly playful grilse just touching my devon, but perhaps with mouths closed.

Salmon also do this occasionally to flies. One on the Tay and one on the Dee have done to me what trout fishers call 'drowning the fly' – leaping out of the water and splashing down on top of the fly. The two fish in question were hooked a few inches behind and below their lower jaws. This brings us to my debt to my Record Books in respect of fly fishing. My early statistics made manifest the relative inefficiency of single hooks (No. 1s and little Low Waters.) compared with doubles (Low Water and Hardy Short-point). My fly ratio did work its way up from forty per cent. In the earlier years of doubles, its seasonal fluctuations were between fifty-five and sixty-five per cent.

Analysis revealed, however, something which I could not have predicted, and would doubtless have mis-remembered without the recorded figures. Comparison of the results with single hooks and doubles showed that the latter had produced a significantly higher percentage of abortive pulls. I found this surprising. I had, however, benefited because the percentage of losses by HCO had declined from twenty-five per cent to nine per cent. The conclusion, which I recorded in *The Field* in 1967, was: 'the moral is that I ought to try to find a fly hook which will reduce mere Pulls as well as HCOs.' Perhaps, unknown to me, Colonel Drury had then started his experiments.

After pooling results for the last seven seasons, including 1976, which has given me only nine salmon, my fly fishing ratio shows lack of progress: fifty-eight per cent (111 from 191 offers). This, however, includes a season of exceptional inefficiency. In 1973 I landed on fly only thirty-five from seventy-five offers. That year I followed Harry's example during our week on the Tay, and left a No. 10 Drury on the tail. My records show that on these flies I had nearly as many HCOs as Landed; yet the five offers known to be to the Butcher on the dropper were all landed. Even a No. 10 double hook designed for trout has a wider gape and can get a better grip than a No. 10 Drury.

I am *not* criticising the Drury hook as such. When Tay salmon will take a No. 8, or bigger, it holds them well. Moreover, my figures are partly a reflection on the way I play salmon. For Harry, during the same week, lost few of the fish which took *his* Drury 10. Harry handles his fish more gently. He was trained primarily by the salmon of the Conway, where it is hard to find a boulder, though there are lots in its tributary, the Lledr. I served my apprenticeship primarily on the Tay, full of big boulders and sharp rock ledges, which had lost me so many fish. I had learned to apply the maxim of all Tay boatmen that more fish are lost through anglers being too soft, rather than too hard, on the fish. I still think that this is true unless one is using the smallest of flies.

Since 1974, there has been some sign of recovery. Thanks to the Butcher, my fly index has averaged just over sixty-six per cent (thirty from forty-five offers). Admittedly, as statisticians would say, this 'sample' is too small to be 'statistically significant'. Still, I put my money on the inexpensive Butcher.

I could go on producing statistics *ad lib*, but enough is enough to explain and defend my fetish. It provides an objective way of testing one's prejudices about the efficacy of different methods.

5
Mixing Philosophy with Fishing

The earlier chapters have contained some jokes. I must now be serious, if only because a fellow philosopher might read this part while browsing in a book shop. I confess that I sometimes feel like a Jekyll and Hyde. Sometimes Mundle the angler considers Mundle the philosopher and says to himself: what a rum lot we philosophers are, requiring innocent students to ask such strange questions as 'How do I know that I have a body, or that other people exist?' Sometimes Mundle, philosopher, takes a critical look at Mundle, angler, and asks how he can justify devoting so much time, which could be spent creatively in criticising others' arguments, to *killing* and causing *pain* to fish which do not harm us? As a teacher of Ethics, among other things, this philosopher has thereby been put on the spot. For one of his moral principles is that it is wrong deliberately to kill, or inflict unnecessary pain upon, other sentient creatures; and like other philosophers he abhors inconsistency, whether in his logic or between his principles and his actions.

Few others find themselves in quite the same quandary, since very few teachers of Ethics go fishing; unless perhaps to escape from domestic problems, or to meditate in what Izaac called 'the fittest place for contemplation'. My interests are an uncommon mix. I have met two Australasian philosophers who have caught trout and would doubtless have sought salmon had they been accessible. I have known only one other professor of philosophy who was a keen game angler. When last I met him, fifteen years ago, he was still at it, though then aged about eighty – Professor A. A. Luce, an Irishman. His many publications include a book in which he mixed fishing with some philosophy: *Fishing and Thinking*, whose last chapter is entitled 'The Ethics of Angling'. (I discuss his thesis later.)

Thus my interests as so far described do not provide a description which applies to only one person. I can, however, do this with the help of one more phrase: 'past President of the Society for Psychical Research'. So far as I know, I was the first student of psychical research to risk ridicule by suggesting, in print, a connection between 'psychic' phenomena and angling phenomena. Some earlier angling authors had at least hinted at such a connection. Thus Viscount Grey, in 1899, wrote: 'It is as if there were some magnetic influence in the angler's confidence, which disposes the salmon to take the fly'. And Ian Wood, in 1957, discussed what he called 'the angler's extra sense'. More recently Falkus has written: 'often I know beforehand when I am going to catch a fish', and he adds that, despite some reluctance, he is drawn to the conclusion that this involves so-called 'extra-sensory perception'. I think it is worth pursuing such possibilities.

Fishing and 'psychic' phenomena

Many philosophers have taken an active interest in Psychical Research on account of the theoretical problems which it poses, but the latter is not part of Philosophy. Far from it. Psychical Research involves the investigation by scientific methods of phenomena which *ought* not to occur according to current scientific theories. The phenomena investigated were labelled 'psychic' on the assumption that they exhibit powers which belong not to a person's brain or body but to his soul. That assumption may well be questioned if only because it now appears that the powers in question are possessed also by animals like rats and hens to which few of us would wish to ascribe a spiritual component.

The puzzling powers which concern us here are as follows:

1. **Extra-Sensory Perception** (ESP), which may be defined thus – acquiring information, not by inference, about things which have not been perceived by any known sense organs.

ESP is sub-divided into: **Telepathy**, if the presumed source of the information is some other mind or minds; **Clairvoyance**, if the presumed source is physical objects; **Precognition**, if the information concerns, and must apparently originate from, future events.

2. **Psychokinesis** (PK), meaning the ability to influence, by means which are not yet understood, the behaviour of physical things, living or inanimate, located at some distance from the agent's body.

The evidence that each of these powers is possessed by at least a few human beings is, I think, overwhelming. The evidence that other species possess at least some of these powers is much less extensive, but it has been accumulating especially during the last decade. A reader who wishes to explore this subject can find a discussion of it and references to many experimental reports in my recent paper 'On the "Psychic" Powers of Non-human Animals' (in *Philosophy and Psychical Research* [1976], edited by S. C. Thakur). Since, in an earlier paper which is reprinted below, I speculate whether salmon are capable of precognition, it seems worth mentioning that some experimenters have recently claimed to show that rodents and birds can precognise, and respond appropriately to, events which have yet to be determined by later emissions of electrons from radioactive material! I shall now present, as food for thought, two papers published in 1958 and 1959 in *Trout and Salmon*. The first concerns the question whether anglers may exercise 'psychic' powers.

I want to discuss what Ian Wood describes in *My Way With Salmon* as 'the angler's extra sense'. Mr. Wood emphasised that in salmon fishing, confidence in one's fly is more important than the fly itself. I too am convinced that the angler's psychological state is of critical importance in determining whether salmon will respond to his efforts. I shall give an example to indicate that this does not apply only to fly fishing. In 1952 I was fishing with my brother. Having recently read the glowing account by 'West Country' of the devons which were named after him (marketed by Hardy Brothers), I had a run of successes with these, whilst my brother caught nothing all week and grew progressively disconsolate. One evening, after landing another salmon on it, I lent him my only remaining West Country devon. He landed a fish within twenty minutes and returned my devon, whereupon I caught another fish with it. Both of us were now convinced of the deadliness of these lures, and next day we motored to Edinburgh to acquire a stock of them. My brother returned full of confidence – and caught five salmon in the afternoon, while I caught none. I may add, in retrospect, that we now consider that the West Country devon, though a good spinner, has no special magic. We have since transferred our faith to wooden devons.

I shall assume without further argument that the angler's state of mind has an important influence on his success. The question I want to discuss is *how* this influence works. One explanation would be simply that if you are confident, you fish well; if lacking confidence, you are unsettled and consequently fish badly. I am not sure whether Mr. Wood accepts this explanation. He seems to recognise that the matter is not so simple: after saying that the angler's control of his tools is 'varied by the mind-attitude of the caster', he adds: 'It is not a case of a quick or slow draw of the fly, but something much more difficult to pin-point; something much more subtle' (p. 20). In any case

I consider the explanation mooted above to be insufficient. The actions of an experienced angler, especially when fishing a big river, are very stereotyped and 'mechanical'. I am sure that I can, and usually do, make my fly or spinner swim through the pool in the same way whether I am feeling fresh and confident, or jaded and discouraged. I suggest that the 'something much more subtle' referred to by Mr. Wood are powers which psychical researchers study – telepathy or psychokinesis (influencing external objects purely by thought or volition). I take this hypothesis seriously and I think that it has some implications for anglers.

Research in telepathy has commonly taken the form of card-guessing experiments. In the earlier psychokinesis experiments, the subject had to try to influence the movements of objects like dice, or, in some cases, of living creatures. The conditions in such experiments must, of course, preclude the possibility that the results are attributable to physical causes of familiar kinds. There are no published records of experiments with fish, but since there is experimental evidence that a man's thoughts or wishes can influence the behaviour of cats and paramecia (microscopic organisms), it seems reasonable to suppose that fish are also susceptible to such influence. I shall by-pass the question, which we have no way of settling, whether such influence should be classified as telepathy or psychokinesis. This would depend on whether it is the *mind* (if any) or the *body* of the fish which is affected by men's thoughts or wishes.

In recent years there have been many experiments designed to determine which psychological factors help, and which hinder, the exercise of these 'psychic' powers. One discovery, confirmed by different investigators, is that confidence promotes and lack of confidence inhibits success. It has been found, for example, that if, before giving them a card-guessing test, you divide a group of people according to whether or not they believe that they can get above-chance scores, the 'sheep' (those who had expressed confidence that they could do it) get an average score *above* the chance level, while the 'goats' (those who lacked such confidence) get an average score *below* (not just at) the chance level. In the light of such facts, I suggest that the angler's confidence is relevant, not, or not solely, because it affects his own physical actions, but because it enables him to exert a 'psychic' influence upon his quarry.

Another feature which has often been reported by psychical researchers is the so-called decline effect. To explain this, during each session, a subject in a card-guessing experiment does many successive runs of (usually) twenty-five guesses. If you pool all the first guesses in each of his runs, all the second guesses, and so on for each of the twenty-five positions in the run, you often find a decline in the scoring level, with the first guess yielding the highest score, the second guess the second highest, etc. Or you may adopt a different method of analysis, taking the runs as your units, and find that the first runs of the day yield the highest average score, the second runs of the day the second highest, and so on. My present hypothesis led me to predict that a similar decline effect would be found in my angling results. I therefore analysed the results of all of my salmon-fishing holidays. I have taken 'contacts' (including pulls and lost fish) as the relevant factor, and have treated a day's fishing as the unit. In nine holidays, comprising sixty-three days' fishing,* I had 111 contacts. For the nine first days of the holiday I averaged 2.7, for the second days 2 and for all remaining days combined, 1.5 contacts. This fitted my prediction. I wonder if other anglers can find a similar pattern in their results?

The hypothesis that success in salmon fishing is due partly to the angler's 'psychic' powers has some practical implications. Psychical researchers have reported that if you induce a high-scoring subject to continue experiments until he is fatigued, his rate of scoring drops to *or significantly below* the chance level. The moral for the angler is here obvious: when tired, give yourself a rest. I applied this maxim last summer with conspicuous success. For the first five days of a salmon-fishing holiday my catches were 6, 2, 1, 1, 0. I decided that this decline might be largely due to fatigue and rested next day to gather strength for the morrow. Then, refreshed, I was *sure* before starting that I would catch fish. I got four of the eight shared by the three rods. I feel sure that fatigue did not cause the decline through making me fish less assiduously. I work harder and longer on a blank day than when I have fish on the bank.

The critic may say: we do not need your far-fetched hypothesis to justify a maxim as obvious as 'Rest when tired'! I shall mention therefore a less obvious implication of the hypothesis. The recommendation of Ian Wood to fish the fly in which you feel most confident suggests that one should rarely change flies. Mr. Wood draws this conclusion. Now many psychical researchers have reported that if a successful subject continues to work for very long in the same experimental conditions, so that the monotony of his task induces boredom, his scoring level declines; but that *any* change in the conditions which revives the subject's interest usually restores his high

* The figures suggest that I fished for salmon on Sundays! Not in Scotland, of course. At the time of writing this, there had been some fishing in Ireland too.

scoring – until the new method in turn becomes boring for him. The moral which I draw is that so long as the angler is not catching fish, he should keep on making *some* changes to sustain his own interest and confidence.

Sometimes the change may be in the method of presenting the lure, but since the scope for such variations is limited, a change of the lure is often appropriate. If I have fished a likely pool with no response, I usually change my tail fly, even if only to the next size of the same pattern. I should agree, however, that the question how often to change one's lure will depend on the individual's temperament. If, like Mr. Wood, your confidence in a fly remains undimmed despite its failure to produce an offer after hours of casting, stick to it. If, like myself, you frequently feel (perhaps irrationally) that a different size or pattern will probably do the trick, you should act accordingly until you start catching fish.

Of the other implications of my hypothesis, I shall mention only one: American investigators have reported that 'psychic' powers are stimulated by a small dose of alcohol but diminished by a large dose. I leave it to anglers who mix drinking and fishing to decide whether the theory fits the facts in this respect.

I shall mention another conclusion (not published) which I drew from the earlier experiments. Analysis had sometimes disclosed not only a decline from the start of a run but also a recovery in scoring level in the last few trials. So that when a subject's runs were pooled, the scoring rate formed on a graph a U-curve. I therefore adopted a private ritual. Whenever I had decided to stop casting, for a rest or a snack, at the tail of a pool or the end of a day, I made three more casts for luck. This ritual has been performed too frequently for record-keeping. I have, however, been surprised, and pleased, by the frequency with which I have hooked a fish with one of those three for luck, especially the third. That salmon which I poached from the Kirkaig was from the third. And in three successive years it worked in the same Kincardine pool – just as I turned about to wade ashore and to start winding in, a salmon took hold of my fly. This ritual sounds like simple superstition. Still, you can try it without telling others.

I shall now report a coincidence. This book was typed and ready to post. I had just told Sheila, for the first time, about my private ritual. I returned to reading J. G. Millais' book, *Wanderings and Memories*, and the first words I read were these:

'We had passed the best of it [a Tay pool at Murthly], and my father had already told Miller [the boatman] to go in, and that we would have lunch. But that last cast is often the fateful one, and in this case it was so, for just as I raised the rod to take in the line, there was a slow boil and I struck'.

This fish, which weighed over 46 lbs, was the biggest that he ever caught. Now what had led me to tell Sheila about my secret was that I had just finished reading Millais' account of the capture of a 36½-lb salmon at Stobhall. The boatman had told him that they had completed fishing the tail of Eels Brigs Pool 'as I gave my final cast. At that moment the rod was nearly torn from my hand, and the reel screamed . . .' This fish was Millais' second-largest salmon. Perhaps I need not have been for twenty-five years too shy to divulge my ritual?

My second attempt to stimulate discussion was entitled 'Do Salmon Foresee Drought?': I have read that salmon run unusually early and in unusually low water at or before the beginning of a prolonged drought, as if they know what is coming in the ensuing months and are seizing the chance to run while it is still possible.

If this is true it presents a fascinating problem for the scientist. From what signs could the salmon 'infer', more efficiently than the meteorologist, what the weather will be like for months ahead? Or are they exercising 'precognition'? Perhaps it is premature to ask such questions, for the first step should be to determine whether this generalisation about salmon is supported by sufficient evidence.

There has been only one desperately prolonged summer drought since I took up salmon fishing. That was in 1955, when, after a dry spring, there was virtually no rain in Scotland from the middle of June until mid-September. That year I caught a grilse in the Tay on 15 May, unusually early, and during June there was an exceptionally heavy run of fish averaging 15 lb when the water was very low; and this lasted throughout the last three weeks of June, when normally the lower Tay is virtually empty of large and fresh-run salmon.

We cannot, however, generalise from one instance. I should like to know whether other salmon fishers have often observed the same phenomenon. If so, I should urge that an ichthyologist (fish-biologist) like Dr. J. W. Jones might seek quantitative evidence, by collecting data about net catches for rivers with summer runs for the months preceding droughts, and comparing them with the catches in the same months in normal years.

This subject preoccupied me in 1959 because we had a prolonged drought in North Wales beginning at the end of April. As was reported in *Trout and Salmon*, the Conway had a record catch in April, and the Welsh Dee showed an unusual pattern of behaviour, where, 'in spite of low water, a good number of fish ran up in May'. And in the Ogwen more salmon than usual ran early in low water in May. I am still wondering what prompts the salmon to do this early running, and I hope that some authority will make investigations.

Apparently the same phenomenon recurred on the Tay in 1976, when the drought went on until mid-September. The Stobhall boatmen told me that their catches were exceptionally good in June and desperately poor in July. I was very innocent in 1959 – thinking that the Ministry of Ag. and Fish. would reveal the figures for net catches of salmon on *individual* Scottish rivers to a mere ichthyologist. He would probably have to become Prime Minister first. These attempts to start discussion, or even some research, were totally unsuccessful. It may be that the purchasers of Sporting and Country journals buy them for their excellent photographs or their advertisements, or perhaps for their River Reports.

Propaganda *a la* Russell

I regard Bertrand Russell as the most important philosopher of the twentieth century. He accomplished his hardest work when young. He devoted many of his later years to propaganda, mainly for a very important cause: trying to stop the human species from doing things which would cause its own extinction. I propose, in a very modest way, to try to follow his example and canvas support for another good cause concerning a different species. I reproduce below the unedited version of an article recently published in *The Scotsman*.

Let's Save our Scottish Salmonidae

The trout are not a problem now that so many come from fish farms to be 'taken' shortly after being 'put'. The danger is of the extinction of our salmon and sea trout. Anglers and biologists have been warning about the crisis and its causes for over a decade. The general public seems unaware or unconcerned. It is more than time that they woke up, if only because of the economic losses.

There is still time to get action if we can get the message to the politicians. Some causes of salmon mortality are beyond our control – the capture, mainly by Danes, of half-grown fish in Arctic waters, catches measured in tens of thousands of *tons* per annum; the disease Ulcerative Dermal Necrosis from which those which do reach our rivers have been dying in large numbers during the last decade. But some important causes could be eliminated by some simple legislation.

Politicians will, of course, ignore such an issue so long as it does not threaten to affect their (re-)election. So those who care must do just that: threaten. We Scots are well placed to exert pressure because we are due to get some devolution. Let us make it clear to all prospective candidates, for Westminster and later Edinburgh, that one necessary condition of getting our votes is a firm promise to enact some needed changes in the Law. 'The salmon vote' ought not to include only 'the anglers' vote'. Apart from conservationists who recognise it as wicked to let a species die out, a lot of Scots depend for their bread and butter on the silver fish. The other nations in the United Kingdom do not owe what we do to these fish, on the hope of catching which so much of our tourist trade depends.

What changes are most needed? I submit that the top priority is to curb commercial catches, with deadly, invisible-to-salmon, nylon nets, in our coastal waters and our tidal estuaries. It is child's play for the netsmen to scoop out *all* the salmon from the long narrow tidal reaches of a river like the Earn. They do, from 5 February until 20 August. In the eighteen years up to 1970 (I regret that civil servants are slow to release such statistics), 95 to 97% of the officially recorded Scottish grilse catch was taken by the nets. These fish run during our holiday season, the summer tourist season. The proportion of larger summer fish which is net caught must be at least as high.

Now 1970 was before our British summers became continuous droughts, throughout which many salmon wait in or near estuaries for the flood which never comes; making it so easy for the netsmen. I expect the net catch to be 99% for 1975 and 1976. This gross inequity (surely an iniquity) compares with something like a fifty-fifty share between nets and rods in England and Wales!

The Tay is the most prolific salmon river in Europe. The netsmen's over-efficiency is now reaping its foreseeable results, for them too. Net catches on individual rivers are closely guarded secrets. But at least a moan has now appeared in print: 'Where have the Tay Salmon Gone?' – a headline in the *Dundee Courier* (21.8.76). The Tay Salmon Fishery Company is quoted: 'Our catches are between a third and a quarter of last year.' And the previous year was another drought summer when they almost got the lot.

If netsmen must be restricted, in their interest as well as that of others, anglers too should accept some curbs. Let us earn the title 'sportsmen'. Why not take two leaves from British Columbia's law book: forbid anglers from selling salmon, and limit their catches. (There, it is four per rod per day.) And a leaf from the River Conway's book: there, only cocks (males) may be killed in the autumn. A six-inch male salmon parr is pleased to deputise in fertilising ova. I would also like to see prawn fishing banned now that its abuse has turned some of the best fly waters into knacker's yards. This too would need legislation, since some proprietors who let their beats are interested only in the number of salmon caught, which determines the market value of their fisheries.

Some anglers have become defeatist about the salmon's coming extinction. Prematurely, I hope. Perhaps unfairly, I have no hopes for the Labour Party which still seems to labour under illusions: that game angling, like owning and running race-horses, is a rich man's preserve; that netsmen are 'workers', but not that much larger class which includes club anglers, ghillies, the staffs of fishing hotels, and of fishing shops, etc; and it seems to ignore the economic facts, notably that what people spend in the hope of rod-caught salmon much exceeds the market value of the netsmen's fish, plus the profits of their employers. (According to rough and out of date estimates published in *Trout and Salmon* [February 1977], what anglers paid solely in rents, on the average for 1971 to 1975, was £200 in July and nearly £50 in August for each salmon caught!) If the prejudices which I attribute (unfairly?) to Labour were truths, presumably Conservatives would be pressing for action. Are they? Perhaps behind closed doors. Maybe there is hope in the fact that David Steel, the Liberal's new leader, is an angler. Perhaps the Scottish Nationalists will be the first to grasp this nettle. If so, they may get my vote, though I do not want Home Rule (yet).

In the last decade, a drastic decline in seatrout runs has afflicted almost all of Britain. The causes are not yet clear. I suspect the increasing doses of increasing numbers of poisons discharged into coastal waters. For the seatrout, we must, I think, demand an urgent increase in scientific research, more hatcheries, and of course, reduction in pollution.

It may be untimely to ask for any increase in public spending. We Scots, however, are stuck with the prospect, a certainty sooner or later, that North Sea oil will accidentally pollute our seas and shores on a scale unprecedented. This gives us some right to ask that a little of the wealth coming from this source shall fund conservation of the wild creatures which still share our land and its waters. Not only to provide hunters with quarry. Surely other creatures too have a right to some *lebensraum*.'

One result of publication of the above was that I was sent a weighty document – the Official Report of the Scottish Standing Committee's Parliamentary Debates on a Bill, now the 1976 Act, concerning our fresh-water fisheries. This confirms my suspicion that prejudices linger in the Labour Party. One of its MPs said: 'The salmon by and large are fished for by *very wealthy people* . . . the trout are fished for largely by *working people*.' (My italics). I got a shock, however, to discover the ignorance of those who were piloting this Bill through Parliament – the Under-Secretary of State for Scotland, and the civil servants who had briefed him. Here is one example:

Under-Secretary: 'As far as I know, salmon do not require any great expenditure – they either come up the river, or they do not. *No restocking is involved*.' (My italics.)
Mr. Corrie, (MP) 'There is great expense in restocking'.
Under-Secretary: 'Of salmon?'
Mr. Corrie: 'Yes.'
Under-Secretary: 'It shows that improvements are being made, *if we have reached that stage*.' (My italics.)

Brown, Malloch, Calderwood and Menzies might well turn in their graves. On the Tay, the Stormontfield salmon hatchery started operations in 1853. No wonder Her Majesty's Government made so little impact on the Danes. The latter may be amused, knowing that many of the immature salmon which they massacre in the Arctic have originated from our many hatcheries, and that none originate in Denmark. Her Majesty surely deserves better-informed negotiators.

One of the anomalies in our new Fisheries Act suggests that the Scottish Office lacks maps. This Act does not follow Lord Hunter's sensible recommendation – to divide Scotland into thirteen or fourteen areas for the purposes of improving and regulating fresh-water fishing. The Act makes the administrative unit 'a catchment area'. This equates the Tay, whose catchment area comprises about a tenth of Scotland, with each burn, however tiny, which flows directly into the sea. The North-West coast and the Western Isles have thousands of them. Perhaps HMG did not relish the task of trying to enforce on wild Highlanders a law under which a trout fisher could be prosecuted; so worded this law so that it does not make sense up there?

I was unfair to the Conservatives in that *Scotsman* article. In 1971, they published a White Paper (Cmnd. 4821, now out of print) which proposed adoption or adaption of all the central recommendations of Lord Hunter's Committee, whose final report appeared in 1965. The 1976 Act has simply ignored its recommendations which do not concern trout. This is sad as it recommended what is surely the rational method of controlling salmon catches: that in each river the commercial catch be taken, at one place only, by means of an electrified grid or a weir. The fish traps would enable running fish to be counted and a certain proportion of them would be left to proceed upstream. This proportion could be adjusted in the light of the relevant factors.

If anyone thinks that this is impracticable on a river as big as the Tay, the answer is that this system has for long been practised on two much larger rivers – the Shannon in Ireland and the Columbia in the United States. On smallish rivers it would be easy to adapt the method used on the Drowes – where there are two passages, each of which takes its turn in forming a fish trap. Apart from safeguarding the survival of the salmon, the Hunter proposals would render unnecessary much manual labour, for they include, as a corollary, the abolition of netting of salmon in the sea on and off our coasts. Any reader who does not recognise the urgent need for action should read Antony Netboy's books, if only to learn how many countries have destroyed or decimated their runs of salmon.

The ethics of angling

When opponents of blood sports challenge me to justify my indulgence in fishing and shooting, I try, if possible, to change the subject. I was once cornered at a Philosophy Department party. After the dining and wining, someone started a new game. Each of the teachers had to make a speech on a subject chosen by a student. Mine was about shooting as well as fishing. It took me unawares. After a long pause, I sang, or tried to, A.P. Herbert's song, which includes the words:

> 'It's all for the sake of the bird
>
> . . . .
>
> I give you my word
> A respectable bird
> Prefers its career
> To be stopped by a peer
> And not by unmannerly poachers.'

Netting the Tay estuary. *Cowper of Perth*

Above: Loch Morar, where one needs a boat.

Below: A wadeable Grampian hill loch. *A. A. Murdoch*

A critical stage of the fight with a Spey salmon. *Arthur Oglesby*

Harry trying the Lucky Hole.

As I sat down, much earlier than anyone expected, I realised how inappropriate was the suggestion that I was a peer, incognito. Still, I was their Professor, and they had to move on to the next victim.

I try to avert this moral challenge because I still feel its force. One does get hardened to it (insensitive?), but I still hate the killing part. The first time I killed anything bigger than a fly, I was ten years old. I threw a stone towards a rabbit, far out of range, I thought. I hit it on the head – stone dead. My father was with me. He said that we could not eat it because it was about to have babies. My father seemed proud of my marksmanship, but I had nightmares about those baby bunnies which had never seen the light. A sense of guilt still stirs, not much when hitting a cold-blooded fish on the head, so quickly done; but very much if I know I have peppered a bird.

Professor Luce, who was also a Doctor of Divinity, evidently had the same sort of conscience. He had the courage to answer the moral challenge, at any rate as an angler. (He was a shooting and hunting man too.) His answer was not obviously outrageous. He did not, like Descartes, claim that the human race comprises the only species of animals whose members possess consciousness and can *feel* pain. He did invoke the Bible and remind us of certain fishermen who became fishers of men. He did not, however, endorse the arrogant view that God made 'the beasts of the field' and 'the fowls of the air' for us to use – to eat, harness, put in zoos, and destroy when we feel like it. The crux of Luce's argument does, however, hinge upon biblical authority – Genesis (IX, 2 and 3), according to which 'every moving thing that liveth shall be meat for you'.

'Those verses', he wrote, 'give the primal permission to kill for food . . . Man has the right to kill for food. It is the law of nature'. Well, it is indeed *a* law of nature that all species do in fact kill for food. (Herbivores kill plants.) Luce's guilt-feelings surface when he adds: 'The right to kill for food, however, does not confer the right to kill for fun or amusement'. Apparently Luce's moral education was even more puritanical than my own. Presumably that was the source of the curious passage which follows.

Notice that the phrase 'killing for fun' is, of course, applicable to the most vicious or perverted kind of sadism. But what about 'fishing for fun'? Luce got himself into a dilemma: fishing for food is our God-given right, but fishing for fun is morally wrong. To try to avoid paradox, he produces a piece of sophistry worthy of Plato: 'We do not often have to fish to get food. Nonetheless we do fish *for what is food*, and we do not fish, save *per accidens, for what is not food*. Those facts make all the difference when the morality of our angling is challenged.' (*His* italics). I invite you to re-read the quotations (or the whole passage on pp. 183–4 of his book), and ponder the implications.

Fellow philosophers could have a lot of (sinful?) fun criticising this passage. I shall confine myself to saying that it does not ease what is left of my conscience. Fishing for fun, or, in other words, trying to catch fish because you enjoy doing so, does not strike many anglers as being sinful, whether or not they or their dependants are hungry. I am disposed to the view that it would be morally more praiseworthy to fish with barbless hooks and *not* eat one's catch, but put them back alive as 'coarse fishers' normally do. (It is, of course, unfair to transfer the word 'coarse' from the fish which they catch to their captors; and some of the species in question, like the graceful dace, could be called 'coarse' only on account of their gastronomic qualities.) Anglers normally eat their catches, because this gives them *pleasure*. (More sin?) I have escaped sufficiently from the influence of John Knox to regard fun and pleasure as good things. For me, a burden of fish is not a burden of sin.

I cannot then still my conscience by Luce's method. Admittedly I have not often caught more fish than my family, friends or benefactors could eat, with the aid of refrigeration. Actually my family has for long been so bored with salmon that, when I fetch from the freezer even a piece of smoked salmon, it is my dog who shows most pleasure, knowing he gets the trimmings. It would therefore be humbug for me to pretend that the motive from which I go fishing is to feed people. If that were so, I would be crazy not to adopt a more effective means of achieving this end. With what it costs in rents and subscriptions, rods and tackle, petrol and tips, etc., I could feed an army.

Sheila has not read Luce. Her moral convictions coincide, however, with his. She expresses his thesis more briefly: 'If you don't eat it, it's murder'. She once made me eat a pike. I was apprehensive, but the wine and herbs enabled me to do my duty by the remains of that brute.

Some will expect an angler who also teaches moral philosophy to say about angling something 'philosophical' in the most popular sense of this word. I regret, however, that I cannot improve on Izaac's advice that anglers should 'be patient, and forbear from swearing, lest they be heard, and catch no fish.' It was, of course, the fish which he thought would be shocked (and put down) by bad language.

The kinds of pleasure for which we fish

This chapter was to have ended there. Then I realised that I had done it again – evaded a moral challenge with a joke, as I did to those students who could not then answer back. Though I get no pleasure *from* killing, be it fish or anything else, I do it and cannot justify it on account of need. And I do fish for pleasure. I try to evade the challenge because I fear that those who make it would not understand my answer, not being acquainted with anglers' pleasures. Communicating these to them may prove as hard as explaining the pleasures of music to the deaf. I shall try, though I know that I cannot match the answers given by others, like Izaac and Lord Grey; and I know that nearly all anglers will regard Luce and myself as squeamish dons.

According to some philosophers, like Plato, Descartes and Kant, the ideal to which we humans should aspire is existence as purely rational beings contemplating abstract ideas. For them a man's 'flesh' obstructs, and his 'animal desires' pervert the spiritual being which is his true self. Even our senses which reveal the wonders of this world are scorned, for disclosing mere 'appearances' and not the realities which lie beyond. I lack sympathy for any such world view. Whatever realities may lie beyond the things which we can see and touch, why should we not savour to the full the beauties of this world? Presumably our *human* nature is God-given, if you believe in Him; so why not accept it and try to fulfil it? Whatever else we may be, we are members of the animal kingdom. As such we are indeed unique in many ways – the extent of our ability to reason and communicate, our aesthetic sensibility, our powers to create (and destroy). But, like it or not, some of us have inherited a hunting instinct; and *homo sapiens* would not have evolved had our ancesters lacked this instinct and not learnt skills to fulfil it.

Opponents of blood sports seem unaware of the fellow-feeling which grows in hunters towards their quarry, unaware also that those most concerned to conserve wild creatures and their habitats commonly have and sometimes indulge this hunting instinct. (Two of the best books on shooting wildfowl were written by Peter Scott.) When young, an angler's only joy may be the more primitive excitements of hooking, playing and landing a fish; but only a sadistic lad would get an extra kick from hitting it on the head. Are there, however, any anglers who are not, or do not become, naturalists? Of course they still savour those primitive pleasures, but they find that there is so much more to gladden their hearts.

John Stuart Mill divided pleasures into two categories: the 'lower', 'the bodily', and the 'higher', 'the pleasures of the mind'. He then faced the problem: how are we to decide which pleasures belong to each category? He gave an astonishing answer – we must each accept the majority view of a panel of experts; the experts being people who have enjoyed each of the pleasures to be compared. Suppose that we adopted this odd decision procedure, surely all anglers on the panel would rank their pleasures among the 'higher'. Conceivably the panel, if ill-chosen, might contain a majority of chess fanatics whose angling experience consisted of unsuccessful float fishing in canals. If so, all game fishers would reject their verdict in favour of chess; and they should dismiss as silly Mill's premise that each pleasure is *either* bodily (and not mental) *or* mental (and not bodily). Anglers' pleasures cut across Mill's crude classification.

Admittedly angling yields some 'bodily' pleasures: in exercising one's muscles, in mastering and applying skill in casting, etc. There is some satisfaction in working well your fly or bait without any other rewards. This gives me, sometimes, as much as one per cent of my pleasure in fishing. It is harder to measure our many other pleasures: the thrill of hooking a fish, the anxious excitement of playing it, relief if one lands it, a pause to admire it. I find it a strain on language to call such pleasures 'bodily'. But even if we did, surely much more than half of the anglers' pleasures *are* 'pleasures of the mind'. These include, of course, the interest in studying the moods and habits of fish and acquiring the cunning to outwit them; but there is so much more.

Three classes of pleasure may be distinguished: (1) the pleasure of fulfilment, (2) the pleasures of anticipation and pursuit, and (3) intrinsically pleasurable states of mind. Classes (1) and (2) presuppose that one has some pre-existing desire. Class (1) comprises simply the satisfaction of getting the object or achieving the goal of such a desire. To get this kind of pleasure it matters not *what* is desired so long as the desire is fulfilled. You may want money, amass a lot, yet fulfilment of this desire may leave you unhappy (perhaps worrying about your investments). Class (2) includes the pleasures of making progress towards your goal, of hope for, and anticipation of, what you crave. Class (3) includes states of mind which often come unsought and which may elude us when they are sought: joy, tranquility, a sense of awe or wonder, aesthetic pleasure, amusement.

I cannot speak for all anglers. There may be some (Falkus?) whose only motive is lust to land fish after fish. For them a blank day must be pure frustration. It seems clear, however, from angling literature that such anglers are not the norm; that many besides myself savour the pleasures of anticipation and pursuit, and find delight in the sights and sounds and scents experienced by the waters they love. A secret source of happiness glows warmer in me from Christmas time – anticipation of my spring week on Deeside. Thereafter the call of Stobhall is rekindled and imagination dwells on those pools, the majestic trees, the rose-bay willow herb, and, of course, the fish. An angler's memory is a magic lantern which projects so many enchanting pictures. We have the luck that our recreation takes us to beautiful places in the gladdest seasons of the year.

Outsiders have some odd conceptions of fishing. Some picture it as day-dreaming with half an eye on a float. Some, more informed about game fishing, assume that a keen angler attends only to his fly or line (or float). As if his visual field were as narrow as a telescope, as if he were blind to the trees and the flowers, the birds and the hills! Well admittedly he should, and usually does, pay heed to the fly or the line. Still the panorama which fills his visual field can also fill his soul. Are non-anglers unable to notice anything not in the very centre of the field of vision? Some do not credit me with this ability. Some of my passengers have seemed nervous that I combine driving a car with so much bird-watching – as if I cannot attend to the road in front as well as the birds and the scenery. They seem to be only half assured when told that I have not crashed yet. In any case, one need not gaze at a view all day to imprint it indelibly upon one's memory.

For Izaac angling was a restful recreation. For some of us it is more strenuous but still, as for him, it is also a *re*-creation. If pressed to explain the pleasure 'for' which I fish, I could reply, sententiously but truly, 'spiritual refreshment'. Some find this in Churches. For others it is only out of doors that they find a deeply felt communion with nature. Anglers who, while plying their art, have partaken in such communions know why Wordsworth called ours 'the blameless sport'; and why we would ask for no 'higher' pleasure.

There is a moral issue not raised by Luce about which I do feel strongly. Some sportsmen are not sufficiently tolerant towards our fellow predators. It is worse among shooting men. It has pained me to see uncommon birds shot, whenever in range – little owls, sparrow hawks, buzzards – any supposed enemy of game birds. I think this is wicked, as well as illegal. Why treat all birds with hooked beaks as *our* enemies? Surely it is better to have fewer pheasants than kill the remaining raptors, survivors from poisons like DDT. To turn to anglers, I have seen a passing heron shot because, I was told, herons eat some trout and salmon fry. And otters are still hunted (or shot) lest they kill a few salmon. In much of this country, the otter is on the verge of extinction. Why grudge an odd fish to such a charming creature, which, unlike us, depends for survival on its skill as a fisher. Moreover, the eels which they eat would consume far more salmonidae than they do.

One of my most exciting experiences when out with a rod was otter-watching. I had just seen a couple of salmon up in the throat of Ogwen's Long Pool, when I noticed that young eels were running. I stood and watched the procession wriggling up-stream. To my astonishment an otter following them swam past underwater a few yards below my feet. Surprisingly the salmon ignored it as it passed close by – safe in the knowledge that it much prefers eels? The otter emerged, sat on a boulder to munch an eel, and luckily did not look downstream. Then off up-stream it went, a bulge in the shallow water. I hurried after, getting closer. Each time it paused on a rock to knock back another eel, I froze. I was within ten yards of it when we 'met'. There was no bush to screen me and it knew that I was not a tree. For over a minute, both motionless, we looked each other in the eye. Then it slipped underwater and disappeared. Either its holt was near or it broke all otters' records for underwater swimming.

6
Some Sources of our Pleasures

From new and familiar waters

I cannot imagine being a one-*method* specialist, unless I had been educated on chalk streams, about which so much has already been written by dry fly purists. Few of us have the chance to achieve their purity. Far more of us are free to choose whether or not to specialise in fishing one particular water, or type of water. Though my own taste is for variety, there is a case for being that type of specialist. If you concentrate for decades in a single river or beat, or on some choice reservoir or a few of them, you should be much more successful there than we non-specialists. For an angler familiarity breeds the opposite of contempt. It may be ten years since you hooked a fish at a certain place, yet every time you repeat that cast you expect it to happen again. You will, of course, enjoy some variety – of weather, hatches, catches, etc. And one lifetime is not enough to learn all that there is to be known about even one fishing water. This is obviously so for a beat on a salmon river, where the lies and taking places vary with changing temperatures and water levels, and quite often from season to season as the winter floods reshuffle the boulders and gravel.

Plato invited us to believe that one's soul keeps returning to earth and that before each rebirth one is offered a choice of alternative wombs. I cannot believe this, if only because the theory could scarcely explain the fall in Scotland's population and the rise in England's. For surely all Sassenachs who had, in previous lives, been game fishers would choose a womb located North of the Border. (Except perhaps for former chalk stream purists.) I, for one, would choose a home where I would graduate as a ghillie rather than one which would probably bind me to a southern city for nine-tenths of the year. If such a womb were vacant, a former angler would, of course, choose one from which he would inherit a slice of river loved by salmonidae and a silver spoon large enough to rent the best fishing elsewhere when he felt like a change. But even if Plato's fancy were fact, it is now too late for such posthumous aspirations. An egalitarian society now seems certain for Britons of future generations.

Those who read fishing books must sometimes sigh at the thought of the countless rivers and lakes where they will never wield a rod. I do, despite the fact that I have had the luck to become close friends with some first-class waters, and from time to time had the chance to explore and to make passing acquaintance with others. It leaves a wound when one loses or finally parts from such a friend, as when I lost Lareen and left the Ogwen. Such wounds, however, heal when one still has a few good friends or the chance to make some more. I can well understand a specialist being content with one or two intimate friends. I cannot, however, conceive of an angler willingly reverting to this state after making many such friends and acquaintances.

No fishery gives of its best throughout the whole of the season. The ideal life for an angler would involve freedom to visit a series of waters, each at the time of its fishing prime. Before the trout are ready, a hardy (and wealthy) salmon man has a wide choice of early rivers from January until Easter. He can end his season on the Tweed throughout November, so only in December need he give his rods a rest. If also addicted to the trout, he is spoilt for choice in May and June. These months are over-generous: the ideal time for tempting salmon with little flies, yet also the time when the trout are fighting fit and most avid for many sorts of flies. For the rest of the summer and autumn there are plenty of waters shared by seatrout and salmon, many not far from lochs where trout will continue to take. Who can blame Thomas Stoddart for making game fishing a full-time occupation? 'Man, I'm an angler' he replied, when asked about his career. University teachers can scarcely complain that their occupation leaves too little time for fishing. Yet sometimes I have felt frustration in May and June – at never being free to depart for a week with the rod amidst the pristine foliage and flowers. No chance to dap on the great Irish lakes, or even to meet a May-fly. Of course such thoughts are banished as soon as the seatrout and summer salmon start to run.

In defence of diversification, I would stress the pleasures which can come from brief encounters, including some which did not yield a fish. Like Loch Coruisk or Sandwood. Take my day at Sandwood. This Sutherland loch had been high on my target list for years, for several reasons: its remoteness, a friend's account of a day there catching seatrout and losing salmon, the romance woven round it by several writers, including even the reported sighting of a mermaid in Sandwood bay. (See *B.B., The Autumn Road to the Isles*, p. 80.) To fulfil this goal, I stayed for a few days at Kinlochbervie hotel. Reaching the loch by the devious track took nearly two hours of walking. Then Sheila went off to explore the coast. With a fresh west wind I spent more time rowing than fishing. Still, by 5 p.m. I had drifted most of the water – expecting a response to every cast, but without an offer, or even seeing a rise. It was a perfect fishing day, so I was baffled, having heard and read of Sandwood's 'numerous seatrout'. We took our tea in the ruin of what must have been the loneliest croft in the country. Sheila innocently asked 'How can seatrout get into this loch?' How indeed. I walked down to the sand-bar to show her the 'small river' of which I had read and which she must have overlooked. It wasn't there! The loch was seeping into the ocean below the sand. The top-most tide mark nowhere reached within a yard of the top of the sand. That summer, at least, only a flying fish could have entered Sandwood loch from the sea. This discovery was not a source of pleasure. It was the view from the sand-bar which made my day. It explained why Seton Watson had described it as the most beautiful place on the mainland of Scotland. Atlantic rollers pounded the silver sands curving north and south below the machair which fringed the rocky coast. Inland beyond the loch rose lovely Bens dappled by sun and cloud.

That sight was a treasure. Still, I did later reproach the hotel for charging myself and others on the higher scale for seatrout plus salmon lochs. The point was taken. I got a free day on a lochan which did have an exit. Though it looked an impossibly weedy tarn, it gave me an unexpected salmon which took the tail fly on my seatrout cast, and managed to keep two dropper flies clear of the weeds. This extra day meant a night in a tent instead of a cosy bedroom. We drove south to Laxford Bridge. At least I might look at this famous river, like a cat at a king; but where could we site our little tent? At last we found the only place between the bridge and Loch Stack, a small expansion of that narrow road. The Duke's river guards must have been in wireless communication. As soon as the tent pegs were firm in the gravelled ground, they converged upon us. We were mobbed by three jeeps and four or five well-tweeded Highlanders. They could see the rods inside my car. A peremptory order to depart was given by the man who carried a rifle. I confess that I lost my cool, and exploited racial prejudice. I expressed surprise that they would take pay from a Sassenach to evict fellow Scots from part of the King's highway; and suggested that they fetch a policeman. Embarrassment was manifest. They melted away speechless, and left us in peace.

From still waters

I have written much more about rivers than lochs and must try to redress the balance. Admittedly running water holds for me a special fascination. The ancient Greeks ascribed a guardian spirit to each grove, hill or spring. I find it quite easy to think like this of rivers. They seem so much alive, each with its own 'personality'. I cannot feel thus about large lochs or lakes, where an angler has to sit in a boat and almost all of his field of view is filled with water and sky. This kind of fishing is exposed to the 'chuck and chance it' jibe. When the trout are dour, it can get monotonous casting one's team of flies.

Wade the River, Drift the Loch is the title of one of MacDonald Robertson's books. On some lochs an angler is required to drift in a boat. If so, and the risk of becoming storm-bound is small, I prefer to be my own boatman. But given the chance I much prefer to let others do the drifting and wade loch as well as river. Then you can get acquainted with the distinctive characters of bays, promontories and weed beds. With the wind at your back and with any luck, you will find places where trout are feeding on insects blown off the bank behind you. Then you can choose which fish to try to tempt. And if you move slowly and quietly, one small bay may provide an hour's excitement before all the fish are 'put down'. And it is not hopeless even in dead calms if fish are still feeding. You can stand in the water, wait for a rise within range, then drop a dry fly near it. And when the trout are wholly dormant, it is much more comfortable lying on heather or grass than sitting on a boat seat. Boat fishers often drift (too fast) down water within easy range of the bank; for the best depth for fly-feeding trout is fairly shallow, and a wise boatman keeps his craft away from the deeps. Indeed it is common to see a boat fisher casting his flies right up to the shingle. Why then bother with the boat?

To wade the loch, breast-waders are best if they need not be carried far. Though one rarely wishes to wade chest-deep, there is less risk of shipping water. Moreover, you can sit on a boggy bank with a dry posterior. When climbing to lochs which lie high in the hills, the less you carry the better. For such forays I adopted a compromise. My canvas waders were made when tough canvas was available. (They had to be tough for their winter use – sitting on salty rocks while waiting for wildfowl.) The feet of the waders could be renewed. It was in the crutch that they finally sprang irreversible leaks. I then converted them to 'crutch-waders', by cutting them at that height and adding belt straps. What remained was over six inches longer than rubber thigh boots, and much lighter. Outsize sand-shoes or rope-soled beach shoes deputised for brogues. They proved ideal on many remote lochs. In most of my favourites the bottom was firm, and the shallows deepened gradually. If one were casting from the bank, one's flies would often be in water still too shallow. Using crutch-waders one could cover ten times as many trout.

Normally during trips to the lochs in the hills, one did not meet another human being between the times of starting the climb and arriving back at the car. I recall one exception. I was fishing alone, as Jim was abroad. About midday a little monoplane swooped down over the hill. It proceeded to make circuits, passing extremely close to me wading in the water. During the first two passings, I returned what I thought was the pilot's friendly wave of the hand. I retired to the bank for the next half-dozen circuits since the trout must have been scared stiff. When, after fishing all afternoon, I got back to my car, I found a keeper waiting with the request that I followed his jeep to the home of the landowner. The latter graciously offered me a drink, and then proceeded to business. Since I had been walking across, and fishing from, his land, he invited me to make a donation to a certain deserving charity. I gladly agreed. He then disclosed that he was the pilot of that little plane, with whose aid he had also located my car, and had then 'phoned his keeper from the airfield near Perth. I kept up my annual donation to the charity; and as I felt sure was expected of me, I continued to make an annual visit to that loch. I was not again disturbed by aerobatics.

Those hill lochs might be scorned by most of today's still water men, who are accustomed to catching trout of magnitudes of which I never dreamed. Some of their farm-bred rainbows are salmon-sized. I note, however, that even on the best of stocked still waters, the average catch per rod/day is commonly close to one trout. In view of this I have no regrets that my still water fishing was so very different, despite the modest size of the trout. Not that I bothered with places where hungry tiddlers abound. What Jim and I sought were trout which averaged at least half a pound, and we found plenty of hill lochs which fulfilled this goal. Only on Loch Leven did our average weight run at about one pound. And only on that bread-fed-rainbows loch did the weight run appreciably higher.

But why should anyone scorn a half-pound trout? It is a good size for a frying pan, and, with some bacon, for a middle course. Caught on light tackle and in the pink of condition, such trout provide a lot of fun. And the sport in lochs well stocked with such fish is so reliable, if fished in the best months and not in the worst weather. Later, when fishing for salmon, perhaps for days without an offer, I have sometimes regretted getting seduced by salmon. From mid-May to mid-July on our favourite hill lochs, it would have been inconceivable to fish for an hour without an offer, or to fish for a day without at least one hour when sport was continuous.

At some stage in July we stopped our Sunday climbs in pursuit of trout – when the evening had become the trout's main meal-time. To exploit the latter it was so much easier to spend a week-day evening on Lintrathen or Loch Leven. Of all the lochs where I have fished the evening rise, Lintrathen, enfolded by well-wooded hills, is the loveliest and was then the most productive. Loch Leven was the greatest lottery – and challenge. It must now be less of a lottery since outboard motors have replaced the pairs of boatmen, and anglers must use their own judgement in deciding where to fish. But then so much depended on the boatmen you happened to get. All of them claimed to know which drifts were currently the best. If lucky, you might get full-time boatmen who really knew. But they were outnumbered by absentees from the coal mines (perhaps with their doctor's approval). Jim and I never learned enough about this spacious loch to risk offending our boatmen by spurning their advice. The catches were distributed most inequitably. The familiar pattern was one or two boats returning, each with a score or more, while most of the boats scored ducks. We had our full share of ducks. The challenge remained – you had the chance of twenty or more of the world's most handsome, delectable, hard-fighting trout.

Soon after 6 p.m. you started to get your money's worth. Usually, for all you caught before sunset, you might as well have rested. It was the hour after sunset which mattered. If you were then in the right place, it was indeed hectic. Especially dramatic was the netting of a fish. The method then used is unique in my experience. The net was of the type used for salmon by Tay boatmen, and only a little smaller. It hung on a heavy metal ring at the end of a long and heavy pole. When an exhausted fish had surfaced within range, the senior boatman made at it the sort of swing which a golfer makes with his driver. There was an almighty splash, but then, invariably, the trout swung up enmeshed.

I must confess that we never got an evening score of twenty, and rarely double figures. I know not how some experts reached their evening twenty as there was so little time. The last hour passed so quickly. One was torn away from taking trout to be back at the jetty by closing time. Our only twenty were caught by day. Lucky in the lottery, we got two regular boatmen, keen types who pulled the heavy boat against half a gale all the way to St. Serf's Island. We spent the whole day drifting down its lee shore with no other boat within a mile. It was nice for once to be Top Dogs, but all the credit belonged to the boatmen, for no-one who could cast a fly could have failed in those drifts. Is there, I wonder, any other loch where a cold and strong east wind is so helpful? In case you get a chance to fish this famous loch, I offer two pieces of advice. (1) Whatever other flies you try, reserve the bob position for a Greenwell with its wings tied back upright (a dry fly fished wet will do), and trip it back through the wave-tops until it is almost under the boat. A fish will sometimes lunge up for it at the very last moment. (2) If you can find a copy, learn all that you can from Burns-Begg's book *The Loch Leven Angler*.

From the hooking and the fight

Chalmers reports having read a certain story – and so have I though I cannot remember where – that for a certain salmon fisher, his cup of pleasure brimmed over as soon as he hooked a fish, and he then lost interest and handed the rod to his ghillie to do the rest. History or legend? There is no other fishing story which I find so hard to believe. Could it be a distortion of what Lord Grey has written? I agree with Grey that in salmon fishing: 'The supreme moment is undoubtedly the actual hooking of the fish.' I should, however, omit 'complete' from his following statement: 'A sense of complete achievement and satisfaction is felt merely in the hooking of it'. But all that he adds is this: 'I cannot say the same of the actual playing of the fish. I remember being a little disappointed with the first salmon I played.'

Grey's last comment should not surprise us. He was already accustomed to playing on the lightest of tackle the large trout of the Itchen. Moreover, his salmon fishing seems to have been confined to relatively small rivers, and usually in early spring. In any case, a moment which is supreme is still a mere moment. It belongs to the past by the time its significance has hit you. Surely Jeremy Bentham was right to hold that in evaluating pleasures we should take account of duration as well as intensity. Grey made it clear that he savoured to the full the anxious excitement of the fight; despite the fact that, when prolonged, it may leave one limp, nervously exhausted. For me at least, a battle with a big one makes my day, even if the fish wins.

In the case of salmon fishing it makes sense to demarcate the hooking from the fight. Except for agile grilse which are travelling fast when they snatch the lure, a hooked salmon is slow off the mark. It nearly always takes some time to react to the unfamiliar pressure. It may even let you wade ashore and quietly walk it a hundred yards upstream before it starts to manifest its power. There is no such pause between hooking and fighting any normal trout. As for a seatrout, unless it is aged or infirm, the reel is already screaming by the time your brain records the pull. At what point would a seatrout fisher hand the rod to his ghillie? The hand that holds the rod must be ready at each instant to dip the rod when the fish cart-wheels in mid-air. With a fresh-run seatrout of three or five pounds, the thrill of *each* moment of the fight is surely as great as the first.

Lord Grey, I am sure, would not have felt that initial disappointment had he hooked his first salmon in a large river when the water had warmed up. Early spring salmon are rather slow-moving in rivers being fed by melting snow. And in smaller streams with short pools a fish lacks room to display its powers of acceleration; and surprisingly often it is content to fight to the death in the pool it has made its temporary home – unless in a flood. One of the reasons why I stopped seeking Ogwen salmon on the day of the big spate was the high proportion of breakages, with running fish in raging torrents. When hooked they continued to run, more often back towards the sea. But whichever way they went, it was very hard to stop them from twisting one's line around boulders at the tops or tails of pools. Such days required a line of twenty pounds breaking strain, and determination to let little of it get off your reel. Thus did I break two spinning rods. Yet the morning after the spate, a fish just settling into its new home would scarcely ever try to leave it. One should never generalise from a single river. I have, however, found the same behaviour in Highland rivers twice as wide as the Ogwen. One of my twenty-six pounders committed suicide. Had it chosen to go through the top or the tail of that small round pool, it would have left me forever. It spent five minutes continuously circling around that pool. It must have got giddy. Obligingly, it paused at my feet and let me, dry-shod, lift it out by the tail. A thick-set cock with no signs of infirmity!

To exploit its power, a salmon needs room to run and a strong current to give it leverage. Once in the Tay I caught a summer fish of over twenty pounds. When it woke up it did a 100 yards sprint and beached itself on the opposite bank, though not for very long. Having learned that lesson, it used the strength of the central stream and quickly found a rock round which to tether my line. I locked the spinning reel and lay the rod on the bank; then walked down to the pool below and asked the head boatman to bring up the boat and help. Bob had obliged thus whenever the need arose, but Bob's successor was that lazy, very temporary, boatman. He declined. Back I went to break my line. Surprisingly, the line was slack, and after winding in thirty yards I found that the fight was still on. Indeed it had scarcely started.

'A minute to the pound' is a well-known adage. Is it meant to tell us how long we *should* or how long we usually *do* require to land a salmon? In either case, it needs much qualification. It is, I think, about right for a fresh-run twenty pounder, but if all goes well, five minutes should be ample for a fish weighing ten pounds. As for whoppers, the adage is much too optimistic. That Conway salmon which wore me down for over 100 minutes could not have weighed 100 pounds. Nor could the fish which beat Jim after 3½ hours have weighed 200! I was not there but I heard his sad tale more than twice. After about three hours a helper returned with a long-handled gaff. He got his chance and slid the steel into that huge flank. He made quite a splash when the fish pulled him in. They later got some glimpses of the gaff trailing beside the bleeding fish before Jim's line gave up the ghost. Salmon of over twenty pounds increase in strength *much* more than in proportion to their weight.

Each of my twenty-six pounders from the Tay took over half an hour to land, one of them nearly an hour. In the latter case there was some excuse for the delay. Sinking tip fly lines had just been introduced. I had decided to make my own sinking extension. At the end of a fishless evening I tied five yards of sinking line to my floater *with a hasty reef knot*. I simply wished to find out how it handled, how far I could cast it. I did not then achieve this, since a clumsy trial cast of less than twenty yards did not deter that fish. Half an hour later it seemed to be almost ready for beaching. I then discovered my quandary. Above the sandy beaching bay the bank rose steeply, thick with foliage – and the reef knot would not pass through the rod's end ring. To try to persuade this fish to lie down, I had to keep retiring backwards twelve yards up the bank, craning to catch glimpses of my quarry through the greenery. Whenever I clambered down to get my hand to its tail, this spurred the fish to splash away and make full use of the current. I could not adopt that useful dodge – when leading a fish on to sand or mud, to stir the latter with a boot and thus confuse the fish with clouded water. That fish gave up only when it was too dark for it to see me.

One who has fished the Tay for as long as I have ought, I feel, to have had a forty pounder. Malloch wrote: 'I have noticed in our fish-house as many as forty fish over forty pounds in weight, all caught in one day with the nets.' Only once have I *known* that I had hooked such a fish, but I also knew it was pointless. It took my spinner just above the end of a very long croy at the foot of Eels Brigs Pool. Every large fish that I have hooked there has run forthwith down-stream and trapped my line below the boulder which forms the end of this croy. Only once had I there released the line by wading ashore and then walked out along the croy; but that was a mere twenty-pounder and the river was low. Today the end of that croy was inaccessibly under water, and this was visibly a monster; for before it turned down-stream it leaped high. The spray from that splash spread far and wide. When I felt that familiar scraping of line against rock, I grasped the whole reel, let the line break, and gave a heart-felt sigh.

I once felt 'robbed' of a fish of over thirty pounds, though I did not deserve it, hooked, as it was, by a Toby in the tail. It tore all over the river. When tearing towards me it moved much faster than I could reel in. I gave it lots of pressure, sure that the hold would be worn out long before the fish. But this went on for so long that hope was kindled. The fish made a very late decision to return to the sea. It did not have quite enough strength to reach the outfall from that long pool. Inch by inch I drew it back and in towards the bank. At last it lay still on gravel three feet deep a few yards out from the bank and only twenty yards below me. A modest current was passing through its gills *from back to front*. It was now safe to reduce the strain, for the fish was drowning. To my dismay a helper came rushing up the bank, having seen the struggle from far down-stream. I shouted and waved him back but without success. He did not stop until he panted on the high bank above the fish, excitedly commenting on its size. Thus stimulated, the salmon made one last try. It reached the top of half a mile of rapid broken water. Ten minutes later I wound in the Toby. Such pains are part of salmon fishing. They have their function – to heighten the pleasure of success.

The pleasures of the fight do not depend on getting a fish which deserves display and a photograph. One of my toughest battles took place on the Dee. That fish surfaced early and looked almost as long as myself. For nearly an hour it ran up and down the strong water below the far bank. I thought it would never tire. When at last I beached it, it was indeed huge, but was, alas, a *very* well-mended kelt. Still, that disappointment could not cancel out my prolonged and palpitating excitement. And no fish has given me more sense of achievement than a certain small grilse.

As mentioned earlier, there is a place on Lower Stobhall, which I have christened 'Fail-me-never' – perhaps prematurely. It can be reached only in *very* low water. Since finding that I could get within range of the 'ease' above that mid-stream boulder, I have had only four chances to swim my fly through it. Each time it has been seized with alacrity – thrice by grilse which were landed. Perhaps I should call it 'One grilse boulder', for the chance of landing from it a bigger fish seems remote. Even a strong and intelligent grilse could win its freedom. All it need do is to dash two yards to right or left and use the passing torrent to take it downhill until your backing had run out. If you followed it down, you would fill your waders and perhaps have to swim.

The other fish which I hooked there was in the fifteen-pound class. It cart-wheeled sideways into the edge of the torrent. My desperate attempt to draw it back broke the hook. Even a grilse has to be held with unyielding firmness while you retreat up-stream until reaching the point where you can proceed diagonally down towards the bank. It was my first grilse from that spot which was most gratifying. During that August heat-wave, the river was at drought level. We had been catching an odd fish before and shortly after the morning 'haar' (East Coast mist) had dissipated. Thereafter the sun beat down on water undisturbed except by anglers. That morning I had seen a fish show above that mid-stream boulder. It was an afternoon for experiment rather than serious fishing.

As I knew, the desired position for covering the lie could not be reached by the direct route. I found, however, a devious route. This involved wading straight out across slack water above a groyne, then about fifty yards diagonally up and out on the edge of a deeper channel until it could be crossed, then down and out towards that boulder. When that lie was in casting range, I was nearing the point at which the force of the current would take me down with it willy-nilly. When that grilse took hold I let out a loud 'Yippee' – to encourage the desultory casting by others within earshot. (Or was it involuntary?) Obligingly this fish let me walk it up as I did my slow backward shuffle. It postponed its running and jumping until we were both clear of the danger area. I reached the bank and had just got it into the slack water above the groyne and success seemed assured, when the fly flew back at me. It was only a few yards from the current, and freedom. Yet I saw the bar of silver sink and lie still on the sand about twenty yards out. I cast my rod aside and splashed out, wading more cautiously and ducking low as I got closer. It started to move as my hand approached its tail. Luckily I got a grip and lifted it out of two feet of water. My second 'Yippee' was louder than the first. It was only a five pounder, though fat and sea-liced, but for me at least it was a triumph – the only fish seen that scorching afternoon.

From being a nocturnal predator

According to Lord Byron:

'. . . the night was made for loving
And the day returns too soon.'

Those of us who love to fish by night for seatrout would endorse at least the second line. Some will regard us as eccentric, perhaps even perverted, for preferring to spend some summer nights so differently from Byron. A certain professor was, I heard, suspected by some students of using night fishing as a cover story for the kind of night-life which they most fancied. His wife knew better. She saw the fish in the fridge next morning.

One would need the stamina of a bull to ply a fly rod throughout every night of the seatrout season. I know a clergyman who nearly achieves this feat. (If the river is high, he uses a worm in the dark.) But when I have fished through two or more consecutive nights this has upset my biological rhythms, digestion included. In any case, I have not felt the urge to emulate the clergyman. I have tried to pick the best nights. The lower the river the better the prospects. Seatrout will run in a trickle. New arrivals will still keep splashing in the tail of a shrunken pool. When a fat moon shines high in a clear sky, the night is made for bed – or romance for the youngsters. Seatrout can see flies in Stygian gloom, so for them a full moon provides as much visibility as the midday sun. Even without a moon, a clear starry sky is not ideal. The night will then get dark enough, but also often chilly. What one wants most is the thermal insulation provided by cloud-cover. Then, if the evening air is warm enough for midges and preferably scented with honeysuckle, the night will not get too cool; and the grateful seatrout will remain active till the signals of dawn appear.

People differ in countless ways apart from what gives them most pleasure. For example, in their night vision. Air Forces have devised scientific methods of testing this for selecting crews for night fighters. I have non-laboratory evidence that this ability varies very widely. I once had a splendid duck-shoot, with a flight-pool for every member and guest. One of our team saw only the earliest of the ducks. Another (Harry, of course) would have gone on dropping ducks all night had they gone on flying. Before he gave up, most of the party had nearly frozen while waiting for him. I was the second-last to return. I gathered that my night vision is, at least, above average.

This hitherto unsuspected gift is a boon when fishing by night. A torch shone towards the seatrout puts them down for a time, especially the big ones. So if you smoke, it pays to turn your head shoreward and shield your lighter; and, when you must use a torch to change a fly, to turn your back to the seatrout and use a mini-torch with an added hood designed to cast a beam just wide enough to light your hands when it is held in your teeth and pointed downwards.

Stealth must be one's watchword. By starting too early many spoil their sport, and maybe that of others, at any rate for the first hour which should be one of the best. One should not go by the clock but by the illumination. Well-rippled water can be fished first without disturbing the rest. Some of the shoal from the calms down below will be up there starting to feed or ready to run. If given the chance, it is prudent to spend the first half-hour or more fishing water well-screened by trees from the remnants of the sunset, leaving more open or quieter water until the trees are just dim silhouettes. When wading in quiet water, one should wade inch by inch so that wavelets do not spread across the pool. Until it is really dark, it pays to play and net and kill your fish without changing your stance in the water. It is surprising how you can develop your senses other than vision, becoming a predator guided by tactual and muscular sensations, learning to detect from the feel of the casting if a tiny piece of weed has joined your fly.

Enough of these prescriptions about tactics. The point of them is to provide keys to open the door to unique piscatorial pleasures, in an unfamiliar world. It is not a world which every angler wishes to inhabit. One of the many ways in which people differ is their need for some solitude. Those who feel no such need may describe us who do as 'loners' – a word which carries overtones of disapproval. Yet those who sometimes need to be alone with nature are often quite sociable people; some play games like golf or rummy, and even enjoy a party. For an angler who savours some solitude there is nothing to match a night with the seatrout without human company. He is not, of course, *alone*. He has for companionship the quiet songs sung by water, the sounds of other nocturnal predators, and from time to time the splashing of leaping seatrout and a singing reel.

'Isn't it lonely?' I have sometimes been asked. That is the last word I should choose. I know what it is like to feel lonely out at night. I once got lost in a derelict forest, returning from a new loch where I had fished in the dusk. The walk from car to loch had taken fifteen minutes. I was feeling not only lonely but alarmed after spending over an hour bumping and falling and groping around that forest.

There was also that encounter with the Devil. Smitten with calf love, I wandered all night on the tracks in a Highland forest. About 3 a.m. I had started to retrace my steps when, loud and clear, I heard Old Nick behind me – a clanging noise and an evil bark. When I could run no further and some sanity had returned, another explanation struck me – that a cow had stirred in its unseen byre. But of course one cannot be lonely, or lost or bedevilled when fishing familiar pools.

A seatrout fisher's night can be the source of deepest pleasures – periods permeated by the peace of the night, punctuated by bouts of intense excitement. He does not complain when the peaceful parts are few and far between. This does not happen very often. After the first hour or two, the peaceful spells get longer. Then he can regather his strength for a fight with the shyest and largest seatrout. In the black of the night such a fish may gently take hold of a large lure, drawn in six-inch twitches, past its nose. Then you need not scruple to splash to the shore, hoping that your fly will retain its grip until at last you ease the fish on to the shingle. Now you have earned a drink from your flask, and a little rest until your heart beats more slowly.

Unfortunately, in describing my own night fishing, I must now use the past tense. As Byron might have put it:

> Though the night be *made* for fishing
> And the clouds obscure the moon,
> Still there's no more river roving
> If one's bones wore out too soon.

7
Nearing the End?

What that question mark hangs over is not the end of this book, now obviously near, but two other matters.

The end of an era?

From time immemorial Scotsmen have regarded it as their birthright to fish for their native trout. In theory riparian owners have had a means of curtailing this liberty, but the law of Scotland made it impracticable for them to exercise this right. In the past, Scotland had provided such a wealth of game fishing that trout fishers had ample scope without causing annoyance to salmon fishers. The rights of salmon fishing were of course legally enforceable, and though penalties were light until 1951, it was very rarely that they needed to be enforced against trout fishers. With rare exceptions, co-operation and harmony prevailed. During recent decades angling has become the most popular recreation in Britain (and America). Demand in Scotland has out-stripped supply. Improved roads have made accessible to anglers from the industrial lowlands waters previously too distant for a week-end foray. As a result bus-loads of converts to the sport have been travelling further and further afield. Some were skilled fly fishers like those who ply their art on the upper Clyde. Some were unscrupulous, and would descend upon any loch or river lying close to a road and pillage it, using set lines as well as rods.

The Government has been extremely slow to take action in the light of changing circumstances. It is somewhat ironical that the action which has recently been taken, the 1976 Act, should have been passed by a Labour Government. For it provides for those bogies – landowners – a legal right to prosecute unauthorised trout fishers. The report of the debate of the Scottish Standing Committee makes it manifest that condoning such an un-Socialist measure imposed a severe strain upon many left-wing consciences. A determined attempt was made, during the debate, radically to change this Bill, so that the first clause would start: 'For the purposes of this Act, all fishing rights (for salmon as well as trout) shall be deemed to be in public ownership'. The Under-Secretary of State had great difficulty in securing the defeat of this motion. The main arguments which he used to placate other members of his party were: that it is indeed the firm policy of the Labour Party to nationalise all fishing in Scotland, but unfortunately this has not yet been included in the Party Manifesto; that, in addition to the substantial cost of administering the scheme, the cost of compensating owners of salmon fishing would be in the order of £250 million, and that at a time of financial stringency this would be grossly out of proportion with the public money being allocated for other recreational purposes.

The motive of the Labour Party in enacting this change in Scottish law was not, of course, compassion for the owners of fisheries. The protection offered to the latter is conditional upon all or most of them in any particular 'catchment area' agreeing to provide to the public reasonable 'access' to trout fishing, and it will be for the Secretary of State to decide whether sufficient access has been promised to warrant him in granting a 'protection order' for this particular area. The motive behind the Act is that legal protection of their trout is a bait dangled before the owners to encourage them to increase the trout fishing available to the public (though hitherto *all* of it has in practice been open to the public!) This somewhat illogical Act does at least provide the possibility of preventing the pillaging of rivers or lochs which are stocked or otherwise improved by angling clubs. The most glaring objection is that under this Act, it will be primarily to the views of such clubs that the Secretary of State will listen; and most fishing clubs have a limited membership and long waiting lists – of anglers who will become legally debarred from trout fishing.

Puzzles remain to be resolved. Suppose a majority of the owners of a river system which holds both salmon and trout should seek a protection order. Will a minority of owners, who wish to keep their trout fishing for themselves and friends, be obliged to let the local anglers and others crowd and disturb their best salmon pools? This is the method of persuasion suggested during the debate by the Under-Secretary of State! (p. 34).

It seems clear that this Act will have to be replaced by something more consistent and comprehensive. The reaction of Conservative MPs to the proposed nationalisation of Scottish fishing was predictable. I share the fear expressed by one MP that the relevant controlling body would be staffed by 'geriatrics'. I prefer the organisation recommended in the Hunter Report – about thirteen Area Boards whose activities should be supervised by a 'Scottish Anglers' Trust'. The Conservatives proposed in 1971 that this Trust 'should be formed, developed and run by anglers themselves with a minimum of Government interference.'

Unfortunately, self-government by anglers will not save our salmon – an asset which must now be worth at least £500 million taking account of the gains from tourism, etc. Rents still continue to escalate though rod catches dwindle. Commercial fishers now know the migratory routes of the shoals of salmon approaching our estuaries, but still well outside the five-mile coastal limit. This form of salmon fishing has been illegal since 1962, but because the herring is nearing extinction, hosts of fishing boats using hundreds of miles of drift nets have turned to this most profitable form of poaching. It is idle to outlaw this without providing the means of enforcement – penalties heavy enough to be a deterrent, and enough patrol boats, guarded at night to prevent their being sunk while at anchor. This recently happened at Berwick. Happily this provocation was followed by some convictions, with whopping fines and confiscation of nets and salmon.

The end of my angling?

Unfortunately I mentioned to my doctor in June 1975 a slight but puzzling weakness in my right arm. X-rays revealed badly worn neck bones including a bone broken in infancy. I was ordered to wear a cervical collar for three weeks. This caused a sharp pain running down from the base of the neck. Still, I obeyed orders, as I was told that they were important. Fortunately the last day of the three weeks was only the first of my week on the Tay. That day I was the old man pottering in the boat. Next day I exchanged the collar for my waders, and landed fourteen salmon on fly in the next five days, without pain.

Three days later, however, the new pain hit me again out of the blue and I consulted an orthopaedic surgeon. My trouble was, he said, simple to cure – by five minutes' manipulation under a general anaesthetic. Since then I have been living on so-called pain-killers and other drugs. As it turned out later, the nerves controlling my arms and shoulders had become crushed by the manipulation, especially on the right side. (They have stayed crushed for over two years.) I managed to complete my teaching next session, sometimes giving lectures from a horizontal posture. The local orthopaedic surgeon had advised me to retire in January, but I could not desert my students. He said that he could not help me but that nature should grant some remissions from pain.

So I returned to my native heath, having acquired a house in a friendly village, strategically situated, should nature restore my mobility and pain-free use of my right arm. The new home is an hour's drive from culture in Edinburgh, closer still to the Tay and Loch Leven, and its residents qualify for membership of a club which rents the fishing on three miles of the River Earn.

Unwilling to accept passively the status of medical reject, I consulted Mr. T. V. Winsor of Dundee having heard reports of skills as osteopath, physiotherapist and acupuncturist. After some trial and error, he found a technique which was dramatically successful – 'rhythmic traction'. Without this help it would not have been physically possible for me to write this book. Alas, after three months of being stretched weekly at a strain of 75 lb, the treatment revived lumbago attacks which plagued me for twenty years. I had bust a lumbar disc by driving a motor-cycle too fast over a pot-holed mountain track in pursuit of Welsh trout.

The surgeon who dismissed me as a medical reject had described osteopaths as ignorant and mercenary. On my evidence this is grossly unjust. I would have been an absent host at Stobhall in August, 1976, had not Mr. Winsor worked on me for 1½ hours on *Sunday evening*, and then asked only for his usual modest fee. After that week on the Tay, I wrote the following piece, in the hope of encouraging other disabled anglers.

There must be other life-long anglers whose bones have become so eroded that using their arms can become torturous. I wonder if they have found ways to carry on fishing. I intend to, using extra painkillers, at any rate when I have a chance to catch a salmon. Fortunately my right arm still has the strength to cast, though using it thus, or for carrying or manipulating things, provokes pains which periodically force me to lie on my back. Unfortunately, the muscle-relaxant which gives more relief than 'pain-killers', can be taken only in the evening, as it has a drastic effect on my motor co-ordination, and would make frequent duckings inevitable if I did any difficult wading.

Last spring I proved that I could still catch salmon on a spinning rod. I thought it was an idle ceremony, the act of an April fool, when I put some fishing tackle in the car on 1 April, and got Sheila to drive me, by easy stages, to Deeside. I had told Harry that it was an experiment, and I should probably have to pack up after a day or two. I'd had two Heath Robinson aids made, hoping that they would help. (1) Using the canvas belt from an old shooting bag, I had a hook tied to the leather ends. The idea was that, with this over one shoulder and under the other armpit, when playing a fish the top of the rod handle could be put in the hook which would deputise for my right hand, while I used a left-wind reel. (2) I had the frilly part taken off an old cartridge belt and had a single-hook (designed for hanging coats on doors) attached at each side; the idea being that after each cast I could let the hook take the weight of rod and reel. It was fly fishing that I had in mind, and also a means of carrying a fish (or two) tied to the hooks on my hips.

It worked! Considerate Harry drove me on the first morning to his so-called 'Duffers Pool' (from which in seven or eight visits I had not yet caught a fish!) But he knew that there were fresh fish in the tail. He left me to it, while he fished a lower pool. I had thought I would only be able to fish with a light fly rod, as I would have to hold a spinning rod continuously with my weak right arm. I spent half an hour establishing that I could cast a fly. The conditions were really quite hopeless for flies less than three inches long. The water was high and well below 40°, and an Arctic north wind blew. So I mounted a toothpick glass rod with one of the fat spoons made by Willy Blair, and I concentrated on the bottom twenty yards where some silver salmon had lunged. Almost at once I had a pull, a fish thrashed the surface and was off. Inspection revealed that one point of the triangle hook was blunt. I cursed myself for not inspecting it first, and ruefully sharpened it on a stone. But my luck held, and when Harry returned from fishing down below I was able to give him a triumphant thumbs up sign. It was a modest nine-pounder, but I have never valued a fish more.

It was now established that I could cope on my own, and for the rest of the week Harry fished Dess and left to me the easy banks of Kincardine. Fishing conditions remained very unhelpful. But next morning, I got a fifteen-pounder low down in the Village Pool. I could not have landed it without my device No. 1, as I had to work it up nearly 200 yards of strong water to the only landing beach. During the next three days I was obliged to spend nearly half the fishing hours on my back, but luckily landed my only other offer, a ten-pounder, in the Claypots Pool. The weather did not suit Dess, more exposed to the icy wind. Self-sacrificing Harry caught only one. That fish were scarce was evidenced by the enormous price salmon were fetching in Aberdeen. But what those three did for my morale could not be measured in money. A tooth-pick spinning rod, which I had never used before on big rivers, proved a godsend, as I could support its weight by gripping the rubber button under my armpit.

In planning for the second week of this fishing year, on Stobhall, I decided that I must abandon my treasured 12½-ft Wye rod and Perfect reel, because of their weight. I bought a Bruce and Walker 10-ft CFR (carbon-fibre rod), weighing only 3½ oz. An extension handle allows one to use it double-handed with salmon lines. And I saved 9 oz. by buying a very light reel. I was disappointed when first trying the new rod on grass with a DT9 line, as I could not, without undue effort, 'aerialise' more than about fifteen yards of line; and on the Tay one often needs to throw twenty-five to thirty yards. So I bought a spare spool loaded with a forward taper No. 8 line, as recommended by the makers; and found that with this I could throw nearly twenty-five yards.

On arriving at the Alderns on Monday, for the first week of August, I was dismayed to find that this usually well-stocked beat had been yielding only two or three fish per week during July. I have never before seen so few fish showing in this water, even in May. All week we were dependent on an occasional handful of new fish running through, survivors from the nets which play havoc in drought conditions. What was most unusual this year was that fly fishing did not beat spinning hands down, as is normal in very low water. The first day I had to be content with two, late in the day, on a devon. I was well content with the first, a fresh twenty pounder which leapt around like a grilse, and ran out of the pool as I tottered down the bank in slow pursuit.

My baby fly rod handled a No. 9 line beautifully when it had the water friction to aid the back cast. I was sometimes casting nearly as far as David, for whom long casting is more than a means to an end. I was, however, losing hope of 'blooding' the new rod when it had not bent to a fish by lunch on Wednesday, and Harry and David, expert fly fishers, had landed only three on fly. But then in the Alderns I met a little run of grilse. A pluck suggested a fish missing my dropper, so I transferred it to the tail, and promptly caught two grilse. During the rest of the week, I got two more on fly, and lost a whopper. (This was the occasion when it is just possible that I taught Harry a lesson.) The loss of the whopper was on the only occasion when I reverted to using a little Butcher on the dropper with a No. 8 Drury on the tail. This fish took the dropper and headed for the boulders on the far side of the current. David bawled at me that I was being too hard on the fish, but I know what happens when a big fish reaches those boulders. It did again: a dead line, and after a while, back came the cast with the tail fly weeded.

I did at least learn that week: (1) a danger in using device No. 1 when playing lively summer fish – you cannot drop your rod forward when they jump. I was lucky not to lose any through this cause – I deserved to; (2) using device No. 2 to take the weight of the rod proved unnecessary. It was easier to transfer the rod to my left hand after casting and mending. The hooks on belt were still useful, however, as a means of carrying fish; (3) having to lie on the bank for nearly half the time is not such a handicap as might appear – one selects periods to fish when experience advises that conditions are most favourable, so the 'productivity' of one's fishing hours increases. I was lucky enough to get an equitable share of our collective catch despite my resting so often while the others flogged on.

Re-learning from the Earn

This section was to have been entitled 'My First Earn Salmon'. There remained six weeks of the Earn's season for catching them (or it), before doing the writing. I felt sure that what the newspapers had been calling 'the drought of the millennium' would end before October ended. At least I was right about this. But how *in*temperate can our climate get? Since 23 September I have experienced my first monsoon.

The salmon had then had a month to queue up, down in the tidal reaches. I had expected an enormous run of them during the first flood. So, of course, had the other thirty-nine Club members. My first Earn salmon was to be caught in the pool above and below the graceful arches of old Dalreoch Bridge, only 100 yards from my car. I found that other members naturally value its accessibility; probably not also influenced, like me, by the fact that 'Dalreoch' means 'the King's hunting place'. (They were Pictish kings with their palace four miles down-stream.)

One of the privileges of retirement is that you can pick your time for an hour's casting on your local stream. I could, I thought, afford to wait until the bank by the bridge was less crowded, until the water fell to fly level or at least to a good spinning height, and until some fish had settled in this attractive pool. It is not like a costly week on the Tay when you feel obliged, in any conditions, to cast until you drop. So I bided my time and noted where others swam their worms or tried their Toby spoons. I was, however, much surprised that it was a rare event when a running fish broke surface, and that I witnessed only one such event involving the capture of a salmon – on the worm.

There seemed to be no need for impatience. The explanation must surely be this: that having for so long awaited water in which to run, the fish were racing non-stop towards Loch Earn. My casual overconfidence made me miss my chance. I thought that those first floods were enormous. They were, compared with the drought level when there was as much weed as water. Yet the floods kept getting bigger, the water more opaque, and I saw no more of those rare events. And I had not foreseen that so many Club members would take their summer holidays in October. By mid-October, time was running out and I was counting the days that remained. Now, it seemed, the best chance of meeting an Earn salmon lay in meadows where I had picked mushrooms, and which were now lying below sizeable lochs. Should the latter subside before October ended, surely some salmon which had sought a short-cut to Loch Earn would be there for the taking. But that is not the way in which one wishes to take one's first Earn salmon, even if it lies on royal hunting ground. (As it turned out, the lochs remained until November.)

I had sent to *Trout and Salmon* my piece on Arthritic Angling, hoping to bring some cheer to other victims. The editor asked, by return, for a photograph of the author using his aids for the disabled. An appropriate picture sprang to mind. In his *Salmon Rivers of Scotland*, Grimble has a pleasing photograph of part of Dalreoch Bridge. Its foreground is a charming creature, wearing an ankle-length black skirt and a straw hat at a saucy angle, holding, by the tips of her fingers, a salmon fly rod. I told the editor that I too would be willing to pose as a foreground for the bridge, provided that (1) the camera got more of the bridge into the picture, (2) it was used on a sunny morning (to get the right sun angle), (3) the caption was '. . . playing a *pretend* salmon', for I cannot con fellow members. My plan was to illustrate the use of device No. 1. With the fly cast fixed to a midstream brick, I would be 'playing' the brick with my right arm conspicuously disengaged. This plan too was in jeopardy. (It was accomplished in watery November sunshine. At least the bridge has come out much better than in Grimble's picture.) The danger was that Dalreoch Bridge would collapse into the salmon pool which it had formed before we got a sunny morning, or before the river returned to a level such that it would not look ridiculous to pose with a *fly* rod. The old bridge has withstood the floods for 209 years. The monsoon has ensured for it an early change in status – from Ancient Monument to Ruin. Large cracks have opened below the arches and part of the structure is sliding via the bank into the river.

I am not, of course, complaining about my initiation into Earn salmon fishing. I would no more judge the latter from first impressions than I judged the Dee by that first fishless week. My introduction to the Earn illustrates the sort of game which salmon fishers play, and explains why it builds character. Admittedly, I have formed the initial impression that few other rivers can be quite so character building. It might develop dogged determination too far – into what some would call blind obstinacy. But I, for one, admire the obstinacy of some of the local salmon men. At least one of them has been fishing every free day and evening since February the 1st. He has not had an offer yet, but he knows that one must persevere. I have stopped proclaiming my impatience to get my first Earn salmon. It seems tactless when they know I have had only a few short spells of casting, not starting until the rains came.

I have, after all, had four good seatrout and three fat grayling. And now I know where some shoals of grayling lie, and that the Earn grayling grow really large – up to 3½ lb, I have been told. So I have the chance, and some incentive, to fish even in winter. And perhaps our disorientated climate will continue to give us mild spring weather, for grayling fishing in winter, before the snow and frosts arrive in April. I have also discovered that grayling are delectable, but I must take a bag when next I seek some. My dog likes them as much as he likes salmon. He seems, however, to have acquired a sense of fair play. He ate only one of the three which I left on the bank, leaving one for Sheila and one for me.

Professor Luce would have approved of the Earn. It seems unlikely to tempt one to kill more fish than his family or friends would wish to eat. Izaac too would have approved, quite apart from its suitability for worm fishing, for it is a peaceful stream, its banks flower-strewn in summer. It is adapted to inculcate those virtues which shine so brightly in his fishing book. I am not now referring to doggedness, which he neither exhibited nor extolled. Rather to the virtues of his simple Christian faith – humility and patience, hope and faith. (Faith in future seasons.) And, of course, charity. I have, again, been touched by the charity typical of Scottish anglers. To a beginner on their water, their help and knowledge is freely offered. No need to produce a flask of whisky. Time talking to fellow anglers when the fish are not taking is time well spent. I have learnt a lot about where and how to capture salmon in the Club water when some have settled there, ready to be caught.

Hope springs eternal in an angler's breast. Mine is fuelled by what

Frederick Hill and Grimble have written about the Earn, and by Stoddart's report that in 1835 it yielded over 4,600 salmon. I share Grimble's faith that the time will come again when its salmon will provide some sport throughout the Earn's long season. Since he wrote, that major obstacle down-stream, the Dupplin cruive, has gone. What remains is for fishery owners to buy out the estuary netting rights, then to restock with fry parented by salmon which had run elsewhere in springs and summers. Though he writes with such charm about trout fishing, I cannot accept the unkind comments made by A. R. B. Haldane about the Earn salmon: 'they do not rise freely, but become red and heavy and lazy.' This description may soon apply to me, but is unfair to the salmon. All cock fish become red as autumn advances. None put on weight in fresh water, even when lolling in sluggish pools. Next season I shall try to disprove Haldane's other unkind comments about the fish of his local river, now also mine.

The reforms which I advocate would take time to take effect. Meanwhile, when we get an autumn without either drought or continuous deluge, this will be a lovely place for a leisurely pursuit of salmon. For when I have to lie on my back, I shall have not only clouds or sky to look at. The Greylags and the Pinkfoot geese love Strathearn too. They are back here in late September. The skeins weave changing patterns in the sky; their voices make music of which I should never tire. 'Study to be quiet' were the closing words of Izaac's classic, published when he was sixty. Wise words, I think; at any rate for sixty-year-old anglers, especially for those with well-worn spines.

Postscript: The Earn has relented – during the first freshet after the nets came off in 1977. After only ten minutes casting in Dalreoch pool, I met a fish which played and looked like a Tay springer. Next day, after fishing for fifteen minutes, I had a successful encounter with a second silvery salmon.

Fishing Books alluded to in the text, with the dates of first editions.

BALFOUR-KINNEAR, G. P. R. *Flying Salmon*, 1937.
Catching Salmon and Seatrout, 1958.
A Boy Goes Trouting, 1959.
BARK, Conrad Voss *Fishing for Lake Trout*, 1972.
BLUETT, Jeffery *Seatrout and Occasional Salmon*, 1948.
BRIDGETT, R. C. *Seatrout Fishing*, 1929.
BROWN, William *The Natural History of the Salmon*, 1862.
BRUCE LOCKHART, Sir Robert *My Rod my Comfort*, 1949.
BURNS-BEGG, Robert *The Loch Leven Angler*, 1874.
CALDERWOOD, William R. *The Life of the Salmon*, 1907.
CALLICHAN, Walter M. *Fishing in Wales*, 1903.
CHALMERS, Patrick *Where the Spring Salmon Run*, 1931.
A Fisherman's Angles, 1931.
At the Tail of the Weir, 1932.
CROSSLEY, Anthony *The Floating Line for Salmon and Seatrout*, 1939.
FALKUS, Hugh *Seatrout Fishing*, 1962.
FARSON, Negley *Going Fishing*, 1942.
GRAY, L. R. N. *The Torridge Fishery*, 1957.
GREENE, Harry Plunket *Where the Bright Waters Meet*, 1924.
GREY of Falloden *Fly Fishing*, 1899.
GRIMBLE, Augustus *The Salmon Rivers of Scotland*, 1899.
HALDANE, A. R. B. *By Many Waters*, 1940.
By River, Stream and Loch, 1973.
HEMINGWAY, Ernest *The Old Man of the Sea*, 1952.
Islands in the Stream, Part One, 1970.
HILL, Frederick *The Greased Line on Dee, Don and Earn*, 1948.
H. M. Stationery Office *Parliamentary Debate. Official Report of*

First Scottish Standing Committee. Fresh-water and Salmon Fisheries (Scotland) Bill, 1976.
HUTTON, J. Arthur *Rod Fishing for Salmon on the Wye*, 1920.
JOHNSON, Stephen P. L. *Fishing From Afar*, 1947.
LANG, Andrew *Angling Sketches*, 1895.
Introduction to the Everyman Edition of *The Compleat Angler*, 1906.
LUCE, A. A. *Fishing and Thinking*, 1959.
MALLOCH, Peter D. B. *Life-History and Habits of the Salmon, Sea-trout, etc.*, 1912.
MENZIES, W. J. M. *The Salmon. Its Life Story*, 1925.
Salmon Fishing, 1935.
MILLAIS, J. G. *Wanderings and Memories*, 1919.
NETBOY, Antony *The Atlantic Salmon. A Vanishing Species?*, 1968.
The Salmon. Their Fight for Survival, 1974.
ROBERTSON, Mrs. N. K. *Thrifty Salmon Fishing*, 1945.
Further Thrifty Salmon Fishing, 1950.
ROBERTSON, R. MacDonald *Angling in Wildest Scotland*, 1936.
Wade the River, Drift the Loch, 1948.
SCOTT, Jock See under A. H. E. Wood.
SCROPE, William *Days and Nights of Salmon Fishing on the Tweed*, 1843.
STEWART, William C. *The Practical Angler*, 1857.
STODDART, Thomas T. *The Angler's Companion to the Lochs and Rivers of Scotland*, 1847.
STUART, Hamish *The Book of the Seatrout*, 1917.
THELWELL, Norman *Compleat Tangler*, 1967.
WADDINGTON, Richard *Salmon Fishing: A New Philosophy*, 1947.
Fly fishing for Salmon, A Modern Technique, 1951.
Salmon Fishing: Philosophy and Practice, 1959.
WALTON, Izaac *The Compleat Angler*, 1653.
WANLESS, Alexander Many short books about the use of fixed spool spinning reels.
WARD, Frank *The Lakes of Wales*, 1931.
WOOD, A. H. E. 'Greased Line Fishing' in *Salmon Fishing*, ed. E. Taverner and others, 1945.
See also *Greased Line Fishing for Salmon*, 1935, compiled by 'Jock Scott' (D. W. Rudd) from talks with and papers left by A. H. E. Wood.
WOOD, Ian *My Way with Salmon*, 1957.